INFILTRATING SOCIETY
AND THE CHURCH

Seduction
& Control

By Dr. Alan Pateman

1. *The Reality of a Warrior*

2. *Healing and Deliverance, A Present Reality*

3. *Control, A Powerful Force*

4. *His Life is in the Blood*

5. *Sexual Madness, In a Sexually Confused World (co-authored with Jennifer Pateman)*

6. *Apostles, Can the Church Survive Without Them?*

7. *Prayer, Ingredients for Successful Intercession, Part One*

8. *Prayer, Touching the Heart of God, Part Two*

9. *The Early Years, Anointed Generals Past and Present, Part One of Four*

10. *Revival Fires, Anointed Generals Past and Present, Part Two of Four*

11. *Why War, A Biblical Approach to the Armour of God and Spiritual Warfare*

12. *Forgiveness, the Key to Revival*

13. *His Faith, Positions us for Possession*

14. *Seduction & Control: Infiltrating Society and the Church*

15. *Kingdom Management for Anointed Prosperity*

16. *TONGUES, our Supernatural Prayer Language*

17. *Seven Pillars for Life and Kingdom Prosperity*

18. *WINNING by Mastering your Mind*

19. *Laying Foundations*

20. *Apostles and the Local Church*

21. *Preparations for Ministry*

22. *Developments and Provision*

23. *The Age of Apostolic Apostleship*

BY DR. JENNIFER PATEMAN

AVAILABLE FROM APMI PUBLICATIONS, AMAZON.COM AND OTHER RETAIL OUTLETS

Seduction & Control

DR. ALAN PATEMAN

BOOK TITLE:
Seduction & Control: Infiltrating Society and the Church

WRITTEN BY Dr. ALAN PATEMAN
ISBN: 978-1-909132-00-9
eBook ISBN: 978-1-909132-53-5

Published By:
APMI Publications
In Partnership with Truth for the Journey Books **14**
Email: publications@alanpateman.com
www.AlanPatemanMinistries.com

Acknowledgements:
Author/Design/Senior Editor/Publisher: Apostle Dr. Alan Pateman
Editing/Proofreading/Research: Dr. Jennifer Pateman
Computer Administration/Office Manager: Dr. Dorothea Struhlik
Cover Image Credit: © coka www.fotosearch.com

"Prune Anything
That Stagnates Your
Creativity!"

❖

Dedication

I dedicate this book to the Holy Spirit who alone is able to open our eyes to the subject of seduction and control; to set us free and keep us free.

If the Son therefore shall make you free, ye shall be free indeed.

(John 8:36 KJV)

❖

Table of Contents

❖

Foreword

Life is a type-rope between good and evil; right and wrong, left and right, night and day, light and dark. Only God can bring the right adjustments and balance into our lives that we truly need. Too many extremes exist. When we attempt spiritual freedom, our own strength lacks the capacity and insight that is gained only through knowing the Holy Spirit and the Word of God.

We leave legalism and fall in the ditch of carnality. We leave fornication and end up in religion. We are incapable of staying out of the ditches on each opposite side of the road. The Highway of righteousness can only be travelled down successfully with the Spirit of Truth by our side.

My prayer is that you walk with Him.

Dr Alan Pateman.

❖

Introduction

Do we have any concept about seduction, deception or Control? These stimulate either by the wrong or right influences that confront us every day of our lives. Our upbringing, parents, children or religion, then there's the media, television, Hollywood movies, music, videos and even children's games to stimulate us every day of our lives and pattern our characters!

We have to ask ourselves an honest question here whether as an individual we are totally free from the programming or control that the world throws at us?

Some forms of negative control are so obvious and yet others are so subtle on the surface and seem very innocent, but any kind of *negative* control is eventually destructive.

The thief does not come except to steal, and to kill, and to destroy. I have come that they may have life; and that they may have it more abundantly.

(John 10:10 NKJ)

Television in general, as one author put it, "...*has become a wasteland for Americans.*" A published report summarised a twelve-week prime time period when T.V showed: 2,149 acts of violence, 915 uses of profanity and 2,019 scenes of sex. The report went on to state that; "80% of the allusions to sexual intercourse in prime-time TV in a particular year were depicted as being outside of marriage," (*National Federation of Decency Journal*).

"Some might tend to think that most viewers can passively watch TV without any negative effects. But the mere fact that American businesses spend over $13 billion a year to sell their products indicates very strongly T.V's power of influence. **When the average couple spends 46 hours per week watching TV and only 27 ½ minutes talking to each other,** it's easy to understand why today's marriages are struggling," (*Page 84, Bob Maddux, Fantasy Explosion, published by Regal Books, A Division of G.L Publications Ventura, California USA 1986*).

Basilea Schlink also pointed out that, "children and young people are influenced by New Age ideas through a barrage of fantasy games, videos, films... books, literature... games and toys. Seven of the ten most popular films in the history of filmmaking are classified as fantasy. Heading the chart was 'E.T.' Which has gave rise to a whole new youth culture; 'Star Wars' was in second place... Seventy-five per cent of box-office successes have fantasy themes.

Fantasy books are best sellers, with editions running into millions. Hundreds of titles are already on the market, almost always presenting some form of occultism *(such as communication with the dead, conjuring spirits, clairvoyance, telepathy and levitating objects by the power of thought)* and featuring sorcerers, witches and magicians" *(Pages 8-10, M. Basilea Schlink, New Age, published by The Evangelical Sisterhood of Mary, Darmstadt, Germany 1988).*

More recently the acceleration of things is much starker. With examples such as: Call of Duty - Modern warfare 3, The Twilight Saga, Mafia Wars, Assassin's Creed, Grand Theft Auto and many, many more... which are all modern games and fantasy films that tamper with our present reality. Either we are given to obsession for the supernatural world of witches, warlocks and ware wolves as in the Twilight series and Harry Potter movies or to games where we can take-on alter egos and live in a cyber world where we can indulge in as much violence and sex as we lust *(minus any responsibility or consequence).*

In addition to this there are today's entertainment gurus from MTV of the likes *(and excesses)* of "Lady Gaga" (AKA *Mother Monster),* who currently enjoys a global influence, above and beyond her predecessor Madonna. Famous for creatively seducing hearts and minds with music laced with intoxicating sexuality and unbridled promiscuity.

So between this cocktail of games, films and intoxicating music, an appetite for violence, uncontrolled power and lust is being fed daily to billions of people worldwide, as this saying suggests: "what you feed, you breed." So it's just a matter of time before the consequence and harvest of all this reveals itself *(this then is brought into the church!)*

Nevertheless when it comes to children I do believe that every child has a right to have his or her own imagination stirred and to enjoy a fair dose of mystery and wonder. After all, isn't that what the special world of children is all about?

However what is actually occurring is that **impressionable young minds are being fed with a potentially dangerous overdose of fantasy and magic!** Children and young people need to grow up in a world where they are able to discern and know what is true. They need to know what absolute truth is: what the unchanging standards in life are.

> It was Jesus Himself who declared, *"I thank thee, Father Lord of heaven and earth, that thou hast hidden these things from the wise and understanding and revealed them to babes; yea, Father, for such was thy gracious will. All things have been delivered to me by my Father; and no one knows the Son except the Father, and no one knows the Father except the Son and any one to whom the Son chooses to reveal him."*
>
> *(Matthew 11:25-27 RSV)*

No wonder the apostle Paul commends and encourages Timothy's example of knowing and reading the Scriptures from childhood.

In addition, the New Age movement – which is the primal force undergirding holism – has significantly increased its visibility says, the Authors of *New Age Medicine:* Reisser, Reisser & Weldon *(InterVarsity Press)* preface.

Introduction

"New Age themes weave through popular books films and toys. Shirley MacLaine's books and TV ministries *'Out on a Limb'* thrust reincarnation and spiritistic trance channelling into the limelight. Discarnate spirits such as *'Seth,' 'Lazaris,' 'Ramtha'* and *'Emmanuel'* have become unlikely celebrities on TV and radio talk shows.

A three-year study by Stanford Research Institute International discovered that some twenty million Americans are 'active in ideas ranging from astrology to yoga, to Transcendental Meditation, to parapsychology... to the study of the occult.' Those engaged in such pursuits have been given a rather complimentary but misleading sociological designation: *'experientially inner-directed.'*

More recently, authors and speakers such as Dave Hunt, Johanna Michaelson and Constance Cumby have generated enormous interest among Christians in the New Age movement. The questions they and others have raised regarding the influence of the New Age thinking upon the church have stirred up a storm of controversy."

We must be concerned with the battle for truth, and the battle for the mind of people in today's world. Satan, the god of this world is a master of lies, SEDUCTION, deception, confusion and manipulation *(control)*. What we read, and see, and hear and experience will either rightly teach or poisonously deceive our minds.

Remember your mind is a battlefield were the forces of truth and error *(deception)* wage war.

❖

CHAPTER 1

Spiritual Manipulation

Spiritual manipulation is very common in the Church today. There are people who will manipulate others spiritually by giving false prophecies, visions and words. They do this in order to control and manipulate people giving the impression that they are very spiritual and close to God.

We need to know when God is speaking to us through another. John Bevere touches on this whole subject of false words/prophecy by relating personal and ministry experiences, which you can read in his book "Thus Saith the Lord" *(Page 90, John Bevere, Thus Saith the Lord, published by Creation House, A Division of Strang Communications Company, Lake Mary, Florida USA 1999).*

He says, "You can be defiled by divination through a word spoken in the name of the Lord. *Divination* is the imitation of the divine.

Through Ezekiel, God said of the prophets of Israel:

They have envisioned futility and false divination, saying,
"Thus says the LORD!" But the Lord has not sent them;
yet they hope that the word may be confirmed.
(Ezekiel 13:6 NKJ)

The Hebrew word for *divination* is *'qecem.'* It means 'an oracle,' yet it is not from the Lord. Simply put, these prophets speak their own oracles as though they were God's. Yet the words are not God's but their own. This is another way of describing the imitation or counterfeit of the true prophetic word of the Lord."

The divination defiles and reduces to a state of limbo or barren uselessness. Again, remember God's warning: "Do not listen to the words of the prophets who prophesy to you. They make you worthless; they speak a vision of their own heart, not from the mouth of the LORD" *(Jeremiah 23:16 NKJ)*.

On the other hand a religious spirit operating through a person who is *not in the flow* of the Holy Spirit and may be giving words, which are false, this is basically a conjuring of words, which is witchcraft.

This also includes any kind of preaching and praying, which is slanted to control, rather than to edify. They pray in a certain way, they pray their ideas and solutions; they want you to hear something, so they pray it out. Spiritual manipulation is another term for *"charismatic witchcraft."* Unfortunately it is widespread in the Church. One of the biggest causes stems from gossip!

They bring judgement on themselves, because they have broken their first pledge. Besides, they get into the habit of being idle and going about from house to house. And not only do they become idlers, but also gossips and busybodies, saying things they ought not to.

(1 Timothy 5:12-13)

Sadly, too many people spend their time talking and gossiping about other people's problems. Proverbs 13:20 says, **"He who walks with the wise grows wise, but a companion of fools suffers harm."** We need to be praying for our brother or sister not spreading gossip about them. If there were as much praying as talking in the Church, the Church would not be in such a mess. Instead, we would be having revival meetings, just like in the days of Evan Roberts of the Welsh Revival.

The Devil's Work

While Satan has kept the Church busy doing his work; thousands of people have gone to a lost eternity. We the Body of Christ needs to get our act together and stop the "I" and the "I WILL," being ambushes, full of pride, thinking one can be enthroned, being ambitious in ministry. Trying to gain control by usurping another's authority and being exalted in praise, slandering others in backbiting, giving false *"words"* and *"prophecies."*

How you have fallen from heaven, O morning star, son of the dawn! You have been cast down to the earth, you who once laid low the nations! You said in your heart, "I will ascend to heaven; I will raise my throne above the stars of God; I will sit enthroned on the mount of assemble, on the utmost heights of the sacred mountain. I will ascend above the tops of the clouds; I will make myself like the Most High."

(Isaiah 14:12-14)

We have not been called to sit in judgement of one another; we have been called as disciples, harvests. The people are perishing though the lack of knowledge, while we the Body of Christ are too busy minding other people's business, instead of doing the work of His Kingdom.

"There needs to be a transition of heart-motive and deed," says Roberts Liardon in his Jan/Feb '99 Newsletter. He says, "As we enter into the last year of this Millennium I'm feeling a transition personally and corporately in the Body of Christ. It's a transition in heart motivation and deed. The knowledge of it so consumes me that I speak of it nearly every time I get behind the pulpit.

It's a transition that will loose into the earth a new generation of preachers. I feel the Father is ready to move in the earth to bring about His great harvest. But He is unable to move, as He'd like because after years of training and preparation, the Church is somehow locked in the clutches of this world's system and has lost her willingness to fulfil the great commission.

When a people become complacent about the heart of God, lethargy moves in immediately and the flexibility and mobility needed for end-time gospel obedience is lost. So, God must move by sending His messengers to re-awaken them to the cause.

Look at history and begin to study how God moved upon a people who were bound. Look at the Dark Ages. The Catholic Church stood as the governmental force in the known world, therefore governmental powers bowed to her. Yet, in the midst of all the religious control there was no liberty or freedom for the people. We preach it, sing it and cry about it, but only Holy Fire consumes the actual sacrifice. It's amazing how we can sing, pray and go to camp meetings but never offer up a sacrifice. WE FIGHT RELIGION, YET WE STAY RELIGIOUS."

Religious Control

In Acts we see the Pharisees, the religious group, trying to control Peter and John.

When they saw the courage of Peter and John and realised that they were unschooled, ordinary men, they were astonished and they took note that these men had been with Jesus. But since they could see the man who had been healed standing with them, there was nothing they could say. So they ordered them to withdraw from the Sanhedrin and then conferred together.

What are we going to do with these men? They asked. "Everybody living in Jerusalem knows they have done an outstanding miracle, and we cannot deny it. But to stop this thing from spreading any further among the people, we must warn these men to speak no longer to anyone in this name." They called them in again and commanded them not to speak or teach at all in the name of Jesus.

(Acts 4:13-18)

This was a religious spirit trying to control and manipulate Peter and John; it is **also trying to stop us as believers from moving out in the power of God.** This controlling spirit operates through people; the person it is using is completely under its control. A person with a religious spirit will speak out against that which is of God; they will remain in the last move of God, speaking out against any **New Wine.**

Have you noticed that once Jesus came out of the wilderness *(in power)* – He only went through the wilderness once remember *(good to know!)* but having left the wilderness in complete victory, that wasn't the end of His testing? Temptation will certainly not have stopped beating against Him; especially from those respectable religious leaders of His day – who were constantly trying to trip Him up doctrinally and discredit Him publicly.

Notice how the wilderness was a private temptation, trial and testing period with none watching, only Jesus, the Holy Ghost and the devil knew what was going on. But it was when He was in the public eye and before the masses, that those religious leaders would attack Him.

In ministry for example, it's usually others in leadership with a lot of influence that attack you! They have either a religious spirit or a spirit of jealousy/envy towards you and your ministry. Your increasing influence is a threat to them just as it was for the Pharisees in Jesus day! They were jealous of the public adoration Jesus received. Remember *wherever* there is envy and strife there is every evil practice.

Who is wise and understanding among you? Let him show it by his good life, by deeds done in the humility that comes from wisdom. But if you harbour bitter envy and selfish ambition in your hearts, do not boast about it or deny the truth. Such "wisdom" does not come down from heaven but is earthly, unspiritual, of the devil.

For where you have envy and selfish ambition, there you find disorder and every evil practice. But the wisdom that comes from heaven is first of all pure; then peace loving, considerate, submissive, full of mercy and good fruit, impartial and sincere. Peacemakers who sow in peace raise a harvest of righteousness.

(James 3:13-17)

Also remember that the devil uses those who are the greatest threat to you with which to attack you, in ministry other leaders are often the closest threat. Where every thing you say becomes analysed and scrutinised! This is why it's important to have the wisdom of God and keep walking closely with the Holy Spirit at all times, as Jesus did.

Do you remember the scripture in John chapter eight, verses 1-11? As Jesus was teaching at the temple courts, teachers of the law and Pharisees brought in a woman caught in adultery. They made her stand before the group and said to Jesus, "Teacher, this woman was caught in the act of adultery."

If you read the story you will find that they were not just trying to accuse the woman of adultery but catch Jesus out. This is true when it comes to a religious spirit. It accuses those that are in sin but also those that are looking to bring the Word of the Lord. But Jesus in verse six just calmly bent down and started to write on the ground with his finger and said: "If anyone of you is without sin let him be the first to throw a stone at her."

Jesus knelt down and began to draw on the ground…

This is a perfect illustration, even though the Bible does not say it – I believe that Jesus was having an inward discourse with the Holy Spirit at this time, so He knew the right thing to say. In Psalm 91 God said that He would, **"deliver us from the snare of the fowler…"**

A snare is a trap and we are the ones who can't see the unseen traps laid up for us but the Holy Spirit can. We must trust and rely upon Him, with complete dependency. For it is the Holy Spirit alone who is able to lead us away from unseen danger and *"lead us not into temptation and deliver us from evil…" (Matthew 6:13)*

So it is evident that religious spirits use trickery, set traps *(& use deception)* in order to discredit the truth. **They are jealous of and easily threatened by the anointing on your life,** just as they were with Jesus and tried constantly to discredit Him, but to no avail. As **no weapon fashioned against Him prospered.** We do not need to fall into them either; as Kathryn Kuhlman is well versed as saying, **"We need not go down in defeat for one split second."** Mistakes are one thing – defeat is another!

The life of making guesses and *"accidental victories"* has gone forever when you begin seriously walking step by step with the Holy Spirit. **Living life ON PURPOSE!**

Accusation or Fact

J. Konrad Hölé says, "You will only know the difference between right people and wrong people, by their love for truth. Lovers of truth are always haters of misunderstanding. Those who do not embrace truth will entertain a lie.

Dysfunctional people, always criticise what they never attempt to understand. Never expect everyone else's passion for truth, to be the same as yours. Some people will embrace a lie about you, not because they want to see you fail, but because they do not want to see you succeed, as much as them.

Your enemies will often look like your friends, until you surpass them. You will never know the depth of a person's love; until they can love you when you're ahead of them controlling people that can't own you will despise your strength.

People that listen to gossip - *usually spread it!* A gossip's information is often too weak for them to stand by it alone, so they must discuss it with others, until they find a source of validation. What's sad is that gossips look to the validation of other gossips, as a means of credibility. When information is wrong, having other people who believer it…doesn't make it right" (*Page 4, J. Konrad Hölé, The Making of A Cutting Edge Leader, published by The World Press, Minneapolis, Minnesota USA 1997*).

Let no man despise thy youth; but be thou an example of the believers, in word, in conversation, in charity, in spirit, in faith.

(1 Timothy 4:12 KJV)

"Champions go to the top, with or without, the approval of others. Champions are recognised on the field, but created off of it. Success is not by permission; it's by decision. Only you determine what you settle for. You cannot complain, about what you tolerate. You loose credibility, the moment you are caught justifying disorder. Your habits will deteriorate, long before your success does.

Your conduct publicly, is always a reflection of what you were willing or unwilling to pay the price for privately. Those who have mastered blame will only resent your victories. You can only trust those who did not need you to be at the top, before they could believe in you. Those that only support you in victory will never support you in controversy" (*Page 31, J. Konrad Hölé, You were Born a Champion, Don't Die a Looser!, published by The World Press, Minneapolis, Minnesota USA 1997*).

Breaking Free

When a prophet is sent into a Church and starts to move in the Spirit, the religious spirit will react badly and will try to discredit him.

A religious spirit likes order and rituals and hates change. People with this spirit find it difficult to stay under the anointing and will manifest more and more as the anointing increases.

Note: If you feel that you have a religious spirit controlling your life, you need to be determined to be free of it because while you remain in its control you will not be free in worship, intercession or in the presence of God.

When in a powerful intercession meeting where things are getting dealt with in the spirit realm and then you start to get uptight and fidgety, this possibly is the manifestation of the religious spirit. This is the best time for this spirit to be dealt with, so instead of withdrawing and struggling, start interceding, start warring *(praying fervently)* taking hold of the power and authority which you have in the name of Jesus and bind that spirit. Keep coming against it until it has gone; remember deliverance is the children's bread!

If you find this is difficult perhaps you need help with deliverance, so ask for it? Don't be afraid to approach your pastor and ask for help. If your church does not deal with deliverance and spiritual warfare, then find one that does.

For ye have not received a spirit of bondage again to fear; but ye have received the spirit of adoption, whereby we cry Abba, Father.

(Romans 8:15 KJV)

God does not want us to be in bondage. **He wants us to move in the freedom of His Holy Spirit.** He is the one who gave us the weapons of our warfare; we are not just to read about them, they are there for us to use everyday. Remember that Satan is beneath your feet; he has no authority, no power over you because we are seated in the heavenly realms in Christ Jesus.

❖

CHAPTER 2

Python is Sent to
Strangle our Success!

In the authorized version of the Bible, this spirit of **divination is considered the spirit of python.** Now we will look at the python spirit specifically found in the King James Version were the writer says, "As we were on our way to the place of prayer, we were met by a slave girl who was possessed by a spirit of divination [claiming to foretell future events and to discover hidden knowledge], and she brought her owners much gain by her fortunetelling. She kept following Paul and [the rest of] us, shouting loudly. These men are the servants of the Most High God! They announce to you the way of salvation" *(Acts 16:16-17 AMP).*

And she did this for many days. Then Paul, being sorely annoyed and worn out, turned and said to the spirit within her, I charge you in the name of Jesus Christ to come out of her! And it came out that very moment.

(Acts 16:18 AMP)

But when one looks up the literal meaning of the word divination here it actually means "gateway or entrance to a city." Likewise the same is meant to be true of an apostolic church *(see Ephesians 3:10)* where it serves also as a spiritual "gateway" to a city, for the Word and power of God to flow in.

The Python however sets out to "stranglehold" this particular authoritative *(apostolic)* preaching of the Word so that demonic *(strongholds)* can use this spiritual "gateway" instead.

A Python spirit is similar to that of a Jezebel spirit - but more complex. Jezebel was outwardly seductive as well as ultra super-spiritual; remember she was a false prophetess. The Python spirit on the other hand does not operate as much around sex and manipulation as it does around prayer and the suffocating of leaders *(especially those with true spiritual authority like those in the apostolic ministry)*.

Notice that Paul was the overall leader there, but there were other men of God present, she went after "them" by saying, "these men are servants of the most high God," but it was Paul who got vexed the most by her touting and taunting and it was him who she targeted the most, because he had the most authority there.

However although Paul was greatly annoyed, he still took his time, *(only Satan is in a rush!)* the Holy Spirit is never "anxious" or "worked-up" and will have been waiting for the right moment to cast that spirit out of her! In other words this was not a "flesh reaction" from Paul, rather a spiritual one, and one that successfully brought about her deliverance, to the disdain of her owners!

The Devil is a Master Strategist

As our adversary is a "master-strategist" and "legalist" let's look at the order, pattern and strategy with which this "spirit of Python" went to work in Acts chapter 16. For it is a fact that, exactly how it operated back then is just how it will operate today. No change! Our adversary has no new tricks!

First of all let's look at the significance of prayer. In verse 16 it says, "...we were on our way to a place of prayer," this clearly shows that this spirit was very much attracted to "intercession" especially with those who have true weighty "spiritual authority." It is still true of intercession groups today.

The python spirit first tries to infiltrate the prayer group. Once it can effectively influence the prayer warriors or the intercessors - its aim is ultimately to stop their effectiveness and fervency [see James 5:16 "the effective fervent prayer of a righteous man makes great power available."] Usually any person who is being used by a python spirit loves to be in the prayer meeting and loves to appear highly spiritual and knowledgeable. It's a super spiritual guise!

Secondly let's mention "mammon" as the continuing verses declare that she brought her owners "...much gain." This spirit's influences include that of greed, severe selfishness *(narcissism)* with a sheer love of money *(one of their main focuses in life which is nauseating to-boot!)*

Then there is the flattery and false loyalty seen where it says that she "...kept following Paul" - *(people operating with this spirit often "attach" themselves to Leadership, but their allegiance is false)*. Leaders are singled out and attacked. In fact I would say that this spirit goes "relentlessly" after leadership.

In the passing of time these individuals often create a false sense of security around leaders and while giving the impression that they are very loyal they bring leaders into great "distress." Everything sounds right - they have all the right-words to say, but like someone once said, "... **it's just like trying to wash your feet with your socks on!"** Something just isn't right!

Then there is the loudness aspect to it as seen where it says she, "kept following and shouting loudly." Those who operate like this lack a great deal of discretion and sensitivity! In fact individuals operating with this spirit are often incapable of being sensitive to the Holy Spirit, although they seem very spiritual! They are loud and draw all the attention to themselves and away from what God is really doing. They stir up a false atmosphere and a "forced-sense-of-excitement."

Tormenting and Unrelenting

To follow this they are very tormenting! As seen where it says, "...and she said this for many days." - It is a tormenting

- unrelenting and unyielding spirit... to the point that Paul and the others were **"...sorely annoyed and worn out."** This spirit's attempts are designed to - exhaust - tire out - weaken and drain leadership, especially the man or woman of God at the helm, as with Paul.

Now ask me how I know all this! It was after my wife and I "endured" similar circumstances as these in our own ministry, not just with one incident but several - yet one in particular. From that point on we decided to make a study of this spirit and its major manifestations. Nothing changes in how it operates; all the "out-workings" are the same even if the host *(person used by this spirit)* is different! Therefore our study still remains relevant today and this is what we discovered:

We found that **if this "spirit" (*Python*) is in operation several major things occur: confusion, distraction, diversion, rivalry, competition, gossip, slander and churches just being "incapable" of working together!** And yes! All of this can go off in just one city, town or place!

In fact if you are a leader and this is going on in your town, then you will find that this spirit will "stir up the people" *(sometimes vehemently)* against you! Even others in leadership will get stirred against you. Those relationships you thought were your friends and your allies; who you could work together with; will completely fall apart!

Note: to pit leaders against each other is a special trophy for this adversary, as it is at authority level and is most damaging to a city.

Demanding All the Attention

To continue; those operating in this python spirit like to demand all the attention; they engage lots of false prophecies by declaring the opposite of what God is really saying, therefore divination occurs *(see familiar spirits in 1 Samuel 28:7)*. This spirit will affect everybody not just leaders, even though it goes mainly for the head honcho! Everyone feels its influence, especially if it gains a stronghold in an area.

We saw this first hand in a region where it operated amongst the churches so strongly that eventually things just began to fall utterly apart. It did irreparable damage for some, and others are still trying to rebuild their lives. It causes "madness" *(making people question their own sanity!)* and causes people to "endlessly question" God's will for their lives *(where previously people were generally secure and clear headed)*.

It is when people feel that they have to constantly second-guess themselves, or justify themselves all the time, that things get very intense! And ultimately severe hopelessness sets in. Many in leadership give up the ministry and simply walk away.

This spirit also causes intense "tiredness," a spiritual, extremely strong and overpowering tiredness, because all the mind games drain people of their vital spiritual energy!

Going back to "hopelessness" just briefly, this was one of the major oppressive elements that we discovered in a small town where we used to live. Also this spirit of python was in operation within the whole region making the churches there totally incapable of working together on any real level. And there existed an overriding sense of hopelessness amongst the people we had to minister to.

The place offered profound potential. There was apparent wealth and opportunity and yet so many of the folks we ministered to, were extremely affected by this deep sense of "hopelessness." On the surface an outsider would not detect it perhaps, but living there for some time, it became so obvious and the average person there was really suffering with it. Hope deferred really does make the heart sick.

What often followed in succession was deep depression and disappointments in people and this provoked much murmuring and gossip. In fact in an area where python has a stronghold, there will be MUCH murmuring, complaining and gossip. It affects everyone underneath it influence, but it is targeted of course especially at leaders.

Spiritual Suffocation

Leaders end up feeling so tied-up that they can't move freely by the Spirit, as they want to. There is this overwhelming sense that they better "please" the people so that the murmuring stops, but of course it doesn't! The plan is "spiritual suffocation" which involves "emotional blackmailing" to exhaust, drain and zap the energy both mentally and spiritually.

Python will drain leaders as with Paul, by sending people who appear to everyone else to be "supportive" (*of all their hard work and efforts)* but actually challenge every decision and every move they make; usurping their authority by lifting up their own agenda or the ones who sent them! Then comes the mockery; they try to overpower people by mocking them and showing outward disrespect. Every opinion they have is loud and public. They are extremely VERBAL and designed to be "intimidating." This makes people take sides with it - in fear of reprisal. No one confronts them.

Those who need all the attention for themselves permanently are probably operating with a python spirit. Now I am not talking about basic immaturity that like centre stage like a child does, but we are talking mainly about those who have influence around ministers and who operate in a premeditated manner especially against authority.

Essentially the python spirit takes people's focus and attention from the Lord and puts it on to other things; just as the slave girl did - who angered Paul so much. They go after the "elect" of God, knowing that even they can be deceived.

Finally a python spirits chiefly wants to rule and posses "cities" not just insignificant slave girls! Verse 20 says, "... OUR city." Their agenda is the "city" or "region" and not just the random individual. This spiritual strong hold that we are calling the Python spirit today, aims higher than the average person. It wants to infiltrate and exhaust leadership so that it can ultimately "hinder" the prayers and "squash" the authority that has the potential to stop and overcome its powers!

Note: it is a great victory for our adversary to bring leaders down by making the people question their authority.

❖

CHAPTER 3

Leadership Seduction

There are certain individuals today who assume that they are in leadership when in actual fact they have never legitimately qualified for such position; rather born from ego and hidden agenda than the high calling of God!

People should think of us as servants of Christ and managers who are entrusted with God's mysteries. Managers are required to be trustworthy.

(1 Corinthians 4:1-2 GW)

So how do we recognise such individuals without starting a witch-hunt!? Well they are really quite easy to spot but having said that, what is obvious to the trained eye is not necessarily obvious to the untrained and therefore spiritually vulnerable.

To begin with they are made up of the type of individuals who have for one reason or another been around the church world for many years and have a good grip on Christian "jargon" and "philosophy" yet more out of "head knowledge" and "learnt-behaviour" than of genuine "living connection" with God! Inadvertently they come to believe that they have in some way been automatically chosen to be a *voice* to the Church!

They even suppose that they have some sort of special "supernatural qualifications," and are convinced that they have some "special insights" that we all need. Along with "special authority" to bring "special correction" wherever they feel necessary - even to the entire Body of Christ! So we must not fail to ask them, **"Who are you and who has qualified you to be in such position?"** Once they open their mouths they usually reveal themselves!

What Qualifies a Leader?

To keep things positive let's look at what qualifies a leader rather than what doesn't. According to scripture, there are **two major qualifications** for leadership. **First of all there must be fruit,** fruit of lifestyle and then fruit of ministry. **Secondly there must be recognition and appointment** *(see Acts 5:1-11; 6:1-7; Ephesians 4:11).*

But first we must look for the fruits; it's okay having a big mouth, but where is the fruit!? Here are some scriptures concerning the "fruit of lifestyle" *(Galatians 5:22; Romans 12:3; 1 Timothy 3:1-f; Titus 1:5-16).*

Consider our example in this matter; Paul the apostle, who went through years of "testing" once he submitted himself to the leaders at Antioch. *"They must first be tested; and then... let them serve..." (1 Timothy 3:10)* According to this particular scripture, once the "testing" part stops, the "serving" part begins! As Paul found out, this took considerable time.

It's remains a fact today that in God's Kingdom the way up is always down and the greatest amongst us is the servant of all. It is only the world that glories in arrogance and "ostentatious crowd-pulling" (*entertaining never qualified anyone for leadership!*) **Someone with a servant's heart is not *showy or flamboyant* but humble.** This is a good sign of leadership quality. In fact, for anyone who has genuinely been called to a leadership position within the Body of Christ, one of **the first things that the Holy Spirit is going to deal with is ...*ego!***

Yet as first mentioned above, certain individuals have the ability to "learn behaviour" that seems to be humble when in actual fact it is known as "false-humility." Perhaps we have become so familiar with the false that we no longer recognise the true. True humility is *often* misinterpreted. Therefore the Spirit MUST lead us, without Him we are spiritually dull and cannot see. We have eyes to see and yet cannot see; ears to hear but cannot hear. Only the Holy Spirit can REVEAL all truth to us and keep us spiritually alert (*John 16:13*).

He is the Father's complete provision for us - so that we cannot be so easily misled. But if we choose to walk without Him, to be vulnerable and spiritually ignorant, then no one can be blamed but ourselves! Yet we are meant to be "over-comers" in Christ, not gullible or easily led astray, but spiritual laziness is often the cause of dullness *(see apostasy).*

The Need to be set Apart

Now let us emphasise on the fact that all potential leaders are "separated" or "set apart" by God *(it is never a **natural** selection; as seen in 1 Samuel 16:7)* and this "separation" actually means *"chosen."* Jesus Himself said, *"Many are called, but few are chosen..." (Matthew 22:14),* meaning that not many make it through the *"testing"* part! Yet the few who do are successfully "separated" unto the Lord *(so not everyone who claims to be a leader, is one!)*

While many want the nametag of "leadership" not many want the "costs" or "associated risks!" And while the "separating process" was never intended to be easy, according to scripture; anyone caught "shortcutting" is not legitimate! *(John 10:7; Matthew 7:13)*

Now let's take it a step further still. There are "offices" and "positions of service" mentioned in the Bible, *(1 Corinthians 12:28 NKJ).* **"And God has appointed these in the church: first apostles, second prophets, third teachers, after that ... helps..."** Once again notice that during those first years in Antioch Paul did **not** occupy a "fivefold-office" *(see Ephesians 4:11)* but instead **served** in the ministry of **helps**, only then did he progress to the office of "teacher" *(see 2 Timothy 1:11; Acts 13:1).*

John Bevere in his book "Thus saith the Lord?" *(Page 120, John Bevere, Thus Saith the Lord, published by Creation House,*

A Division of Strang Communications Company, Lake Mary, Florida USA 1999) says, "Not only would Paul be tested in the realm of helps but in the office of teacher as well. When Paul was promoted from teacher to apostle we again see how God chooses and separates those that He wants to fill certain offices or positions."

In Acts 13:1-2 we can see how Paul was listed along with other teachers in Antioch and how the Holy Spirit wanted them to be specifically "separated" unto Him. The appointed time had finally come, the one who had been called to be an apostle all those years earlier on the road to Damascus in Acts 9:15 had finally, after many years *(possibly 14 years)* of testing and loyal service, was he successfully "separated" unto God to be an apostle.

First he was **"called"** then served in **"helps,"** then he progressed to the office of a **"teacher"** and finally the office of an **"apostle."** Why? The reason: Paul was faithful to promote the Lord and not himself *(see 1 Corinthians 4:2)*.

Staying Accountable

Then, having fasted and prayed, and laid hands on them, they sent them away. So, being sent out by the Holy Spirit, they went...

(Acts 13:3-4 NKJ)

Now the emphasis here is twofold; *"**They sent them...**"* and *"**...sent out by the Holy Spirit.**"* This means that to have "official" leadership you need the authentic commissioning of the Holy Spirit alongside "recognition" that is necessary from other leaders. In order to promote Paul the apostle,

God used the established leadership with whom Paul had already faithfully served, during his years of testing and ministry of helps.

Some misguided folks think that they can go around saying, "I am anointed - I don't need anybody else - I don't care what they think!" This sounds impressive to some perhaps, but really it's nothing short of "stupid!" Without recognition from other leaders our own position can never be legitimized only jeopardized. It's vital to work together with others. Having said this, it is also normal to lose any reputation before you gain one! Losing your life, before you save it! Dying to self so that the "person" can be built before the "ministry" and the ego dissolved! *(Jesus had the wilderness for this process but we have a lifetime!)*

Nevertheless when we humble ourselves God promises to raise us up. Therefore to go any distance in leadership and to gain that recognition from other "leaders" this involves humility on our part before leaders. However this doesn't mean that everybody who is in leadership becomes our apostle or mentor!

God never called anyone to be a lone ranger. We must never work alone. There may be seasons where God strips us back, to deal with our heart motives but even in the Adullam cave, David had a small crowd going on *(1 Samuel 22:1)*.

Paul did travel alone at times but not all the time. More importantly he did not "operate" alone or solely under his own authority. He worked in collaboration with other recognised leaders; especially from Antioch and Jerusalem from where he was sent out.

From inception then, it's crucial to remember that it is before God AND men that we must serve. Recognition comes from God first and then from men, but not just anyone. That's why it's important that other "recognised leaders" recognise us before God. Not all will of course; but there certainly should be some! Especially those who God has brought divine connection with. Without this, there is no lasting influence or authority *(sensationalism evaporates; yet true anointing and genuine recognition can last a life time).*

Certainly to begin with and on a continual basis, there must be humility and submission towards others in leadership. God did not use anyone that Paul was not in submission to; instead He used an established authority that had already been set up in Antioch.

God will never undermine the leadership of the Body of Christ just in order to raise up someone else into a position of leadership with no accountability!

So with recognition comes appointment *(ordination)* by other leaders, in other words "confirmation" of certain leadership qualities *(Acts 5:1-11; 6:1-7; Ephesians 4:11).*

However, on the other side of the spectrum there are those who want to lead without first being led. Those who have no intention of ever operating in or out from a place of submission and yet expect submission wherever they go! These types of people have to "assume" leadership, because they have not gone the proper way. Usually in fact they have no recognition except for their own imagination!

47

Their assumptive leadership behaviour operates something like this: they like to have influence *(where possible)* straight at the top. They like to "steer" where they have no authority to "steer." They start by infiltrating a church or group where they have had little if any input, nor developed any real relationship or invested any quality time and yet insist on airing *"unqualified"* opinions. Even their silence suggests something!

They leave people hanging, waiting and wondering, so that even when they are absent, everyone is still thinking about them - almost possessed in their thoughts - something that ends up completely controlling. The result is that a false dependency upon their opinions develops and this is always dangerous.

Having successfully infiltrated and gained trust they begin to draw back, causing confusion and hurt; making others push in even harder towards them. People begin believing that they now "need" their affirmation. However a big characteristic of these unauthorised leaders is that they remain very "guarded" and "safe" about their own personal lives. They only share so much as to get you interested or impressed and then they stop. They withhold information, to make people feel that they have to "earn" their acceptance!

Gaining Intelligence

All the while these bogus leaders are gaining "intelligence" on everything and everyone else, because "knowledge is power" to them. Their "self preservation" goes undetected at first but then it's realised that they "never" give anything away about themselves. They never indulge information about their own lives yet they manage to extract info from others, about *everything*, what they are doing, "how and why," only to use that information to "pass judgment!" They use all information they can get as strategic "ammunition" for such times they feel threatened!

Eventually those around them feel more and more "raped" of information each time they enter conversation with them. They try to resist the urge to "gush" but always give in to the seduction, which induces the feeling of depression, like they are literally "giving their lives away."

The seduction works so well because they give the sense that they are really interested and want to know, but less is always more with these people. The less that is shared with them the better! Their genuine concern is appealing however and they usually succeed in seducing their victim.

The depth of their "concern" is revealed in time, especially when they use that information just to "prove their theories" and issue an, "*I told you so...*" They estimate themselves so highly and regard their opinions as law that they act out of extreme self-righteousness and pride. But they fear exposure! *So they cover their tracks so carefully so that no one tells on them!*

Ever met anyone like this? I am sure that you have. We all have. Seduction is not always sexual. It can be intellectual, informational; anything that makes us feel that we must have what they have. But it's very safe for them to stay aloof, watching and judging everything from the side-lines, endlessly analysing, assessing, criticising but never *doing* anything.

They are too afraid to really commit to anything - that might affect their safety zone or expose them in any way. They don't ever reveal their own weaknesses - but they want to reveal everyone else's! They feel they must "rescue" everybody by "correcting and coaching" them in the things of God! When really the greatest need is theirs! They prey on the vulnerable and it's only a matter of time before the vulnerable eventually wise up!

Most importantly they cannot prove anything; they only have "words!" And yet they indulge in making everyone else feel like they have achieved nothing. Nothing worthy in their sight that is! Regardless of all the proof and genuine achievements!

When they do come across genuine success it *challenges their own theology* so much so that they begin to look for ways to disprove its legitimacy and to prove it wrong. They bide their time; watching, analysing and waiting for "leaked" bits of information that they can use. After all, anyone who is not just like them *must* be wrong...!

This is absurd. Anyone can assume the role of "judge;" watching everything yet remaining unaffected by anything *(anyone can do this!)* People who do this don't want to pay their own price - they'd rather reap the benefits of the risks that others are willing to take! After all, the Bible does say - watch and pray - not watch and "judge!" In fact if you hear someone constantly criticizing others, just ask them when they last prayed for those same people! Their reaction should say it all!

Finally: all of us should be accountable to leadership in one way or another. This stops us getting carried away and helps makes us more careful. We cannot be established alone. Submission is not harmful for us - long term it's more than healthy. Covering - keeps us from being vulnerable and open to attack from the *bogus and false.*

Ultimately, anyone who persistently says "No" to the Holy Spirit - is a dangerous character. **Remember, the misguided always want to steer others!** And fruitless people always have big opinions that *only measure up to their own dreams but not to reality!*

❖

CHAPTER 4

Character Assassination

A dictionary definition for "parasite" is as follows: - "an animal or plant that lives on another animal or plant without giving anything in return..."

Let us continue with this concept of "leadership-seduction" which involves those individuals who impose their assumed and unqualified leadership upon others. Not unlike the parasite in nature or society, these individuals fall into the category of "spiritual - parasite!" Without living off the lives of others they simply don't have a life of their own! And those of us who have experienced this type of indulgence from others will be familiar with the following.

The spiritual parasite is an individual whose interference and activities in the lives of others is never fruitful. Like the opening definition says, a parasite is all about TAKE! They live off the energy, anointing and vision of others; believing that they are entitled to make all manner of "directional – suggestions" as if they were talking about their own lives! And spiritually speaking, they drain the very life source of their victims and when able to live off of these victims for lengthy periods of time, actually begin to claim "ownership!"

Most of us have experienced this in some fashion or another and know that pretty soon they want to be the *umpire of every decision* that is made and demand an explanation when changes have been applied without their approval! When you begin to endlessly "justify" your actions to them, it is then that you must remind yourself that this person is not even in leadership!

In addition, because these people *need* others in leadership to "endorse" them, they arrogantly treat those in genuine leadership positions, as if on an equal footing - to empower themselves all the more!

Note: when people in general see that these individuals appear to have so much sway with others in leadership, they begin to treat them the same way and this is just what they want! They try to hang out with those in leadership all the time; because it is all about appearances!

They want to be seen having spiritual weight, so that their opinions really count. So watch out, not to give them too much valuable time; endlessly talking, because this helps them to establish their bogus "position." We must remember, they are always "positioning" themselves & EVERYTHING is calculated.

Every single conversation, no matter how "relaxed" it might seem, has a hidden agenda attached to it. You must remain alert and not be so easily duped! Especially since they are "masters at flattery" *(seduction)* with their appealing "opinions" about your particular "destiny!"

The Tragedy of Hit-N-Run

So much so, that you actually become convinced they are as committed to your success as you are! No way! In fact their plan is that our success must become "their" success. They are a parasite remember. They will take their fill and then leave. Depending on how much you have to offer, it can be a drawn out affair or a "hit-n-run" experience! Either way they are toxic! In Isaiah it says; "Traitors continue to betray, and their treachery grows worse and worse..." But in his closing verse Isaiah triumphantly states; yet *"He will be glorious in the presence of his respected leaders"* (Isaiah 24:16-23 GW).

Another attribute to their seductive behaviour is that they are consummate "time-wasters!" One sure sign is that they will consume HOURS of your time - yet make you feel that you have consumed hours of theirs! They insist on knowing "everything" and encourage lengthy explanations and justifications! After you exhaust everything – you always wish you hadn't!

Why did they "need" to have all that information anyway? Once again you "explained" your lives away, gushing like you just couldn't stop! *[Then comes the accusation is that you talked about yourselves too much! When all you attempted was to answer their endless QUESTIONING!]* By indulging them in this way, you've simply invited this parasite to dinner!

Another characteristic of leadership seducers: they *always* "disapprove" and like to make you "feel" their disapproval! Oh... it's not in what they say - it's in what they "don't," say that makes you feel it! The pause, the silence, the look - it's the way they posture that helps the impact! And it's the questions they "don't," ask and the information they "withhold" that has the potential to bother you the most! And no matter how lengthy your explanations - they never "satisfy!"

Unquenchable Lust

Remember lust is hard to satisfy and in their seduction, they have an unquenchable lust for information. Knowledge is power. The more you talk, the more they hope you will "leak" some private information that they can "really" use! For those of us who are in leadership, we have to guard ourselves from becoming over familiar with those who are not in leadership. *(We must be careful even with those who are! But especially those who aren't...)*

This type of individual doesn't just want to steer people's actions but also their thoughts, to get into their minds and under their skin. It's a similar feeling to "possession" and "deliverance" only comes when they are cut off *(they rarely eject!)* In fact it's difficult to get free of their manipulations; when we attempt to bring distance, at first they turn on the charm even more, and how could we possibly live without them?! But charm is the flip side of the same coin as nasty! When separation comes, so do the attempts to discredit; *(now they **must** discredit you in order to save-face).*

56

If allowed to continue their influence in your life, these individuals also pursue a position like that of a "personal-spirit-guide," who constantly gives out advice! However the Holy Spirit is the only "guide" we need spiritually speaking, along with genuine advice, from genuine leadership!

Those who are barren cannot pass judgment on the fruitful. Remember people who consistently deny the Spirit don't grow. They systematically refuse to "flow" with what the Spirit is doing and "always" want to suggest a better way... their way! Their "faith" is counterfeit and consists more of humanism - pride - and unbelief than anything else! They always flow cross-wise from the Spirit, even though they insist that they really know the Holy Spirit. They talk the talk - but don't walk the walk.

Even watch how they worship. Is it all about them? Notice that in "everything" these people are consumed with themselves. Not just with the normal insecurities that others face, *(plus a willingness to overcome)*. No! They are completely stuck on themselves, in an unhealthy, narcissistic way. They appear to be always in a crowd but actually they are very isolated and narrow in their thinking; completely convinced they are right about everything.

Our security must be in the Lord. As leaders, these people infiltrate our surroundings usually because of our genuine and healthy desire to succeed - in achieving what God had told us to do. Without this "drive," nothing is ever achieved except apathy and procrastination!

However these people latch onto the *genuine* in order to bring about the *counterfeit*. So be strong and of good courage!

When you try to eject from such unhealthy connections, be ready for a fight! *(The battle belongs to the Lord and the victory is ours).* **The drive to achieve is good, but we must keep it pure. Amen!**

Humanism or the Spirit of God

I warn everyone who hears the words of the prophecy in this book: If anyone adds anything to this, God will strike him... If anyone takes away any words from this book of prophecy, God will take away his portion of the tree of life...

(Revelation 22:18-19 GW)

Admittedly this focus on "leadership seduction" may seem slightly negative, but a subject that must be addressed nonetheless and always better tackled than left. After all, a lot of us have encountered these types of people who either don't want to change or are completely ignorant that anything is wrong *(ignorance is **always** arrogant!)* Nevertheless we still have the option of heaping up "many" teachers to tickle our ears as scripture puts it, with "tastefully designed and politically correct teachings" that only address what we want to hear.

Yet avoiding all things negative is not wise and keeps us shallow and uninformed. Awareness *(not conspiracy theory)* prevents spiritual threats, which arrive on the doorstep of EVERY church group or ministry. No one is immune; *ask me how I know!!!*

So to continue, yes these bogus leaders *(without qualification or recognition)* hate to be challenged - yet challenge is precisely what reveals their false anointing! *(They are easily threatened!)* True anointing attracts "trouble," it comes with the territory! But these individuals have a hatred for all things *"challenge" or "change!"* but it's what reveals insecurity and weakness, like nothing else!

I believe and always have, that the Holy Spirit uses "change" a lot in order to teach us and sometimes it may even seem that the only "constant" in life is "change!" But it is this that keeps us fresh and unstuck!

Note: change is not synonymous with crisis as some folks treat it! And it helps to keep in mind the following: behaviour in the first moments of a crisis reveals who and what we truly believe!

Character assassination is another trait: many of us have had our integrity questioned and it's never pleasant! Generally it doesn't stop with us either but also affects our families, our marriages and every area possible *(especially if we are leaders!)* However it is the accuser of the brethren who does this. [But there is balance to everything and leaders must not use this as a cloak to cover everything by saying, *"...don't question me about anything...!"* No! We must remain accountable; to our flock, to each other and to the Word.]

Bogus leaders never enhance unity and leave a trail of "separation" and "disunity" in their wake: of marriages, associates, and friends; even longstanding relationships, all left in tatters *(see Proverbs 16:28)*. They don't "co-habit" and when they have the opportunity they specialize in "rescuing and then despising!"

Counterfeit or Original!

The Bible speaks of many falsehoods *(2 Corinthians 11:4 + 26)* such as false brethren, false apostles, false spirits, false doctrines and false prophets, to name a few! The point is this: **there is a counterfeit to anything that has an "original!"** *(For example have never seen a counterfeit "$30 dollar bill" or "£9 pound note," simply because there was never an original!!)*

"False-brethren" for instance are those who consistently find something to make an accusation about. They are not unlike "false-witnesses" except they shout about stuff they do witness but don't like! And there's nothing much they do like! The "humanism" that steers them is not of the Spirit of God; they have the uncanny ability to totally "misread" everything!

They easily make a controversy over anything and seek to correct their leaders by saying, *"We don't want to undermine you, BUT..."* Usually these same people have such "delicate" consciences *(no faith)* that they use this to manipulate their leaders to pass EVERYTHING by them first; to the effect that nothing happens without "their" approval!

What all these people struggle with is *humanism* - and more often than not they exalt **"psychology"** *(science of the mind)*, over and above the very Word of God. In fact false leaders love to quote more from their psychology books than from scripture; yet quote just enough scripture to keep it convincing! They offer a complete mix. Mixing the "Word" with anything is dangerous, because it must be kept pure, unadulterated and defined as the true Word of God.

Even though psychology has its place, though limited, it certainly must not be "mixed" with the Word of God; especially where people don't know the difference! *(To qualify this let me say the following: if people insist on using psychology then they must "define" it as such and not mix it with - add it to - or - mistake it for - the Word of God, because pretty soon people in general won't be able to recognise the difference).*

Besides - psychology only applies to the "fallen mind" and not to the "renewed mind." Those born of the Spirit know their mind is *"being"* renewed by the Word of God daily. Psychology only studies the mind in its *"fallen-state"* but it cannot *"renew"* anything! Humanistic reasoning must not be added to God's Word *(see Revelation 22:18).*

Clearly not everyone who claims to be genuine and led by the Spirit is what they say they are... However scripture gives us one main source of evidence to prove or disprove the genuine from the bogus; chiefly "FRUIT." Its presence or absence speaks volumes. If any of us truly walk by His Spirit, there will always be evidence to prove it! There is always evidence to the life of the Spirit *(tongues is evidence of the baptism, fruit is the evidence of the Spirit led life).* Whether it is fruit of character or of ministry, there is *always* fruit where the Holy Spirit resides.

Finally, even though we have looked into the behaviour of the false and bogus - none of this is "personal" or aimed at "flesh and blood," rather spiritual forces that are opposed, hostile or anti-Christ *(anti-anointing, anti-truth, anti-righteousness!)* The anointing breaks every yolk of bondage *(which takes genuine authority!)* **Remember that where the counterfeit can only "question" Christ, the true anointing always "reveals" Him and His Divine Nature.**

❖

CHAPTER 5

Paradox Unveiled

Daniel 11:32 says, "And such as violate the covenant he shall pervert and seduce with flatteries, but the people who know their God shall prove themselves strong and shall stand firm and do exploits [for God]" *(AMP)*.

The King James says, "Corrupt with flatteries." This word "corrupt," in the Hebrew means: to defile greatly, to pollute and profane! The word "flatteries," in the Hebrew literally means: to be smooth, to separate and **divide.** Even like something that is very smooth and slippery like a treacherous spot where one would dangerously slip. Seems like flattery is a dangerous thing to be involved in! *(See Strong's #02610, 02514 & 02505).*

Evidently, flattery caters to the flesh. The Spirit of God's Holiness will never flatter us or lead us to flatter someone else. This is of a wrong spirit. In Galatians chapter 6 and verse 8 it says; *"...For he who sows to his flesh will of the flesh reap* CORRUPTION, *but he who sows to the Spirit will of the Spirit reap everlasting life,"* (emphasis added). In fact anything of the flesh is corrupt. Then the Amplified version says, **"... decay and ruin and destruction..."**

So, it's safe to say that flattery is something, which certainly ruins, destroys, corrupts, pollutes, separates and "DIVIDES" - Concluding that the use of flattery ultimately ends up coursing a whole host of trouble and is very divisive.

Not surprisingly the devil uses this weapon often, but Jezebel also, where in 1 Kings 18:19 we saw how she used flattery to beguile her false prophets, by providing for them and making them to eat at her table. The only motive behind this was to get them to prophesy in favour of her husband. What he wanted to hear, rather than voicing the true message of God *(1 Kings 22:7-8, 23; 21:7).*

> *But there was no one like Ahab who sold himself to do wickedness in the sight of the Lord, because Jezebel his wife **stirred** him up.*
>
> *(1 Kings 21:25 NKJ)*

So what does this actually mean, that she *"...stirred him up?"* If we take another look at the Hebrew we find out that it actually means: *to prick, stimulate, to seduce, entice, move, persuade, provoke, ...stir up.* One way of achieving this is through **flattery *(see Strong's #05496).***

We see in the "Concise Oxford Dictionary" that the word flatter/flattery means: to compliment unduly, over-praise;

gratify the vanity of, **make feel honoured**, inspire (*...with unfounded hope*), exaggerate, ...smooth. Which is exactly what we see Jezebel doing here in 1 Kings 21:7 where she says to Ahab,

> *Do you not govern Israel? Arise, eat food, and let your heart be happy. I will give you the vineyard... (AMP)*

Really King Ahab was sulking here, because he couldn't get his own way. Not forgetting that He was a king who "*... did evil in the sight of the Lord, more than all who were before him*" therefore any "honour" given to him was certainly unfounded and exaggerated! (*1 Kings 16:30*)

Flattery is a False Honour

By protecting *his* interests Jezebel was protecting her own! It's not wrong for a woman to be passionate about her husband, but it's important to go about it in the right spirit. Because **flattery is a false honour**, it will never aid but eventually greatly hinder. True honour comes from a right spirit and correct motives (*Proverbs 31:12*).

It is actually possible for a precious woman, who loves her family with all of her heart to still be motivated by a Jezebel spirit in some areas of her life and be totally unaware of it until the Lord reveals it to her. She doesn't even have to "BE" a Jezebel! And outwardly would probably seem the last person to be branded a "Jezebel."

However all it takes is a few tendencies here and there or agreements/alignments with this particular spirit and you've already been influenced... with a potential to influence! You may not be the power craved, career possessed type, but you could still be controlling your family – and seeing it as love.

Note: For example, "possessiveness" is always more about us than about those we claim to love, more to do with the-fear-of-loss and of pride, than about anything else.

You must see that the Jezebel spirit is one of the strongest influences on the women of our time. It is the spirit of this world and women are being schooled in the school of Jezebel without even knowing it. They are taking on the spirit of this world and its views, and they are doing it by simply "AGREEING" with them *(and this includes Christian women!)*

Let's take Colossians chapter 3 and verse 21 that says, *"Do not **provoke** your children, lest they become discouraged."* We can take a look at the Greek meaning for the word "PROVOKE" and perhaps we can locate ourselves a little here!? Provoke in the Greek language is the word *"erethizo"* which means: to stimulate, especially to anger. Connected also with another Greek word, **"eris"** meaning: a quarrel… wrangling, contention, debate, strife, and variance.

As this suggests, causing strife, wrangling, contention or hard debating is never good, but especially not with our children – it is not God's way of parenthood and it's not His best for our children. He is concerned for them. Provocation, in the negative is always detrimental, especially where our children are concerned and evidently important to God. We are told NOT to do it. He cares about the upbringing of our children because they are the next generation of generals, revivalists and preachers.

It's sad to say that in many homes there is often strife, including Christian families! Wherever the FLESH is in control, there will be "corruption," *(see Galatians 6:8 KJV)* and corrosion or corruption of the family happens when strife is allowed on a consistent basis.

Jezebel at Home

Parents can stir up strife in the home, either the husband or the wife - or both. But we will look at the important role of the wife here. A woman can set the "entire-tone" of the day in her household. She can set the course of her family's day, by what comes out of her mouth first thing in the morning. Good mood or bad...! Hormones or no hormones!

A woman is meant to be her husband's crown and glory *(see Proverbs 12:4; 1 Corinthians 11:7)*; a nurturer, life giver *(like Eve)*, a nest builder and homemaker... but she was never meant to provoke her children to despair or *"EMASCULATE"* her husband, by trying to take his place!

One fact that we can see in scripture is that Jezebel knows how to "STIR" people up! But we are told in 1 Peter 3:4-6 *(see Amplified version)*, that women in particular should not become "hysterical" about anything.

What about true tenderness that is found in the Father heart of God? His is a tender heart so responsive, willing and ever ready to be moved by the needs of His children, *(which is why He is so responsive to intercession).*

Ask yourself a pointed question, "Would God ever treat my family the way that I sometimes treat them?" *(This question has the power to convict!)* Mostly we would say, "NO!" because God is tender and compassionate, firm but loving and always responsive to their heartfelt cries. Mostly He is longsuffering! Never impatient and always kind – He IS LOVE.

God said to my wife on one occasion, when she was getting a little impatient with our small children as they were fussing, *"I want you to treat your children, the way I would treat you..."* Needless to say this took her back and convicted her instantly!

If you look in the "Vine's Dictionary," you will discover that "provoke" means: amiss, to make bitter. *(There is a positive sense to provocation, such as provoking someone into truth, but the "provocation" spoke of in Colossians 3:21 is negative and causes "discouragement," see KJV).*

Provoking clearly "embitters" and "stirs up" what is evil in others, like Jezebel and Ahab in 1 King 21:25, where it says she **"incited"** him. I think all of us at times have incited each other by operating in the flesh and even provoked our children at times; because of various pressures and frustrations *(every parent has fallen short...!)*

However, if this is a continual occurrence in your home, church or work place, *(if everywhere you go there is division - especially against authority & leadership)* then you need to ask yourself some very serious questions! Could it be *YOU* who is causing all this? Do you always get involved in arguments at work? Do you always *HAVE* to have the last say in everything? Do you always stir things up...? Do you find yourself inciting people rather than speaking the peace and love of God into every situation?

If so, then you need to repent of yielding to this spirit and submit yourself back to God and command this Jezebel spirit to flee from your home and your life; to stop influencing you and stop influencing others through you *(James 4:7)*.

It is vital to know then, that when Jezebel goes unchallenged, she can make other people's lives a misery, *(just as she did for prophet Elijah!)* You could be making other people's lives a misery right now. Jezebel intimidates, manipulates and has people running around franticly all the time, either trying to avoid or to please her! She wears them out with her "continual" provocations.

To "stir up" in the Hebrew "cuwth" as we have already seen means: to prick, stimulate, to seduce, entice, move, persuade, provoke, remove, set on, stir up, take away and is connected with another Hebrew word "shayith," scrub or **trash**, i.e., wild growth or weeds or briers *(as if put on the field): thorns.*

Think of it like this, when you incite people and provoke them to anger, *(which we know discourages them)* it's like **"setting-on-them"** every time they make mistakes or things you don't like. Speaking **"trashy" words at them,** sowing wrong seeds into their lives. Again this type of continual manipulation suffocates, which we have all felt at some point in our lives. We must now be certain that we do not become the "one" who does this to others.

Now in order to keep things positive, before doing a *Jezebel-check,* what about doing a *holiness-check?* What tendencies do you display that line up with the Holy Spirit?

For prime example: what fruits of the Spirit are manifesting in your life at this point? It's time to locate your true identity; whether it's more in line with the spirit of this world or more inline with God's holiness!

We do not want to cause the wrong kind of growth in the lives of our families, **where briers and thorns grow up instead of "roses."** What and who you really are will manifest in your children at some point. Not always manifesting straightaway – but *"later-on"* always comes!

Division and Separation

Remember that Jezebel always brought *"DIVISION & SEPARATION."* Many people are capable of stirring up division in their homes and aligning themselves with this spirit completely unawares. And most people who genuinely love their families don't understand why there's constant division amongst them. But if there is something constantly amiss in the atmosphere of your home then you must ask the question why?

The wife alone, for example, has the strongest ability to set the whole tone and atmosphere of the home, more than any other member of the family, yet will it be conducive with Jezebel and the spirit of this world or with the Spirit of God?

Many women find that the more they get upset, agitated or excitable – the more it reflects in the rest of the household. Her moods can cause great unrest in the atmosphere of the home, mostly causing great division amongst the different family members.

If you are struggling with division in your home, do a "Jezebel check" and see if you are inciting any of the members of your family like she did Ahab? It might be your teenage children or it might be your spouse. Put a stop to it and when the strife stops so will the division and everything else that strife brings with it.

My wife believes and often says that there are many tender-hearted women, who genuinely care about people and family, who would be literally devastated if they thought they were in anyway aligned to this Jezebel spirit – even if it was in the smallest way. But we can't afford to be naive about the devil's tactics or about Jezebel in the world today.

It's hard to get away from, unless you totally separate yourself from this world. Like scripture tells us, "...we are in it but not of it..." and that "...we are not to be conformed to this world but be transformed by the renewing of our minds..." *(Romans 12:2)* Why? To literally unlearn all that the world has taught us! In fact we do indeed live in a world that's steeped in **Jezebel's perverse and deceptive doctrine**.

I have a few things against you, because you allow that woman Jezebel... to teach and seduce...
(Revelation 2:20 NKJ)

The Spirit expressly says that in latter times some will depart from the faith, giving heed to deceiving spirits and doctrines of demons...having their own consciences seared with a hot iron...
(1 Timothy 4:1-2 NKJ)

As we have grown up in this world, during our formative years many of our mindsets have already been shaped by her influence whether we have been aware of it or not. The biggest avenue for that of course has to be the *worldly media,* but also the schools. The only way we can reverse this is by pushing into a holy God and allowing Him to make us… **holy as He is holy** *(1 Peter 1:16).*

Flattery is something that makes you feel good, so if you were insecure, you would enjoy being flattered. This opens you up to manipulation and a Jezebel attack. It is good to encourage and bless one another, but flattery in the sense of trying to get your own way or make someone feel that you like them more than you actually do is manipulation.

Jezebel's use of flattery is very subtle; it can bring *damage and division* into relationships. She will set people against one another and her deception brings jealousy, strife and disunity to a once strong unit.

Then, she will do her best to get the prophet to endorse her ministry. She knows that if she can get his endorsement she will find acceptance and will be able to speak into other leader's lives. If you endorse her, she will automatically gain acceptance from other people, so that she can then speak knowledge into situations, which opens the door to deceptions, which will cause problems later on.

The person controlled by a Jezebel spirit will not be obvious straight away. Initially, she appears to be very submissive, but behind your back she begins to gossip, telling people of the things which she opposes. This is to undermine your position and to gain control. She wants you to put her in a position, whereby she can gain greater acceptance, and participate in the leadership. Eventually she ends up controlling and manipulating the situation in the way she desires.

The main areas the Jezebel spirit operates, is in *control and division*. It can do that through many different means, such as division between a man and wife. As soon as submission stops, then an argument starts; Satan gets a foothold and causes division. **The moment you cease to submit, you raise yourself up into a place of authority, which has not been given to you.**

Submitting to Authority

Anarchy is the devils devise for making and keeping a generation powerless and easy for him to control. He convinces them that their power & strength lay in rebellion. **The truth is that rebellion strips you of authority.** The devil knows that he was stripped of his authority to cover the throne of God as a cherub, once he decided to usurp the authority of almighty God.

In his anger, he has been deceiving generation after generation to do the same - to usurp authority. This is the most effective way of making no threat to himself. Rebellion is the sin of witchcraft and there is no righteous authority in rebellion.

When the righteous are in authority (become great), the people rejoice; but when the wicked man rules, the people groan.

(Proverbs 29:2 NKJ)

Why rejoice over righteous authority? Because *"righteous authority"* brings freedom, growth and joy where rebellion only brings bondage. Keeping us bound and living unrighteously, is all he has to do keep **choosing**, rebellion, which keeps us on a course of destruction. The choice will always remain ours to make; the devil can only tempt, lie and try convince us to make poor decisions, but he can't ever MAKE us do anything. If God Himself won't MAKE us do anything, then the devil certainly is not allowed to, he can only try and "influence" us.

We know that God won't MAKE us do anything either, even when it comes to salvation. The ultimate choice of heaven, hell, life or death – rests with us. Not even then will God step in and FORCE us to rescue ourselves. We can see this freedom of choice that He gave to us *(including the seriousness of it)* in *Deuteronomy 30:19* where it says, *"I have set before you life and death… therefore **choose life**… that you may live…"* God therefore will NOT make the decision for us – we MUST to do it for ourselves.

All God does if you notice is strongly recommend us to choose LIFE…*!* That choice will never be taken away from us; the decision will remain ours until the day we die – only then will the choice be gone forever – what we chose while still alive on this earth will stick for eternity, Christ and His blood, heaven or Hell!

The devil knows this very well, we see in the wilderness when the devil tempted Jesus that he knows the scriptures very well. Knows them and is able to twist them and he knows that the power of choice remains ours until the day we leave planet earth through death. This is why we must be fully persuaded *(of truth)* just like Paul the apostle speaks of in *Romans 4:21; 14:5*.

If you're not fully persuaded of truth, you will be more easily persuaded of the devil's lies. Being persuaded of truth daily enables us to make the right kind of choices the devil hates…!

Because of this sin *(rebellion, lack of submission, usurping authority)*, Satan can come in with more things other than division. He *(Satan)* is then allowed to inflict with demonic powers in these situations.

> *But if you have bitter jealousy (envy) and contention (rivalry, selfish ambition) in your hearts, do not pride yourselves on it and thus be in defiance of and false to the Truth. This [superficial] wisdom is not such as comes down from above, but is earthly, unspiritual (animal), even devilish (demoniacal). For wherever there is jealousy, (envy) and contention (rivalry and selfish ambition) there will also be confusion (unrest, disharmony, rebellion) and all sorts of evil and vile practices.*
>
> *(James 3:14-16 AMP)*

It is however within our control as we have seen above, the decision belongs to us, and whether to put things right or leave them alone. Therefore we must choose to repent, put down the flesh, and get rid of that rebellious spirit, by making sure that we come into submission to the Father first *(James 4:7)*.

We must resist the devil when these things of the flesh and sin occur. For example, when the devil attacks with division in a marriage, both people need to pray against it together, hand in hand, quickly as possible restoring the unity in the relationship.

❖

CHAPTER 6

Jezebel needs Ahab

The sooner the Jezebel spirit is recognised and ousted, the better. As the Jezebel becomes stronger, she will have greater influence over the people in the Church. Her hold upon them will be very strong, so when she is removed from fellowship, these people are going to feel extremely hurt and may leave the Church.

They will believe that this person is of God, so they will be very confused, not understanding what is happening. These people need to be counselled and cut free from the demonic hold of this Jezebel spirit.

People, who operate under the influence of the Jezebel spirit, tend to carry a lot of hurts. So you have to be careful how you handle them, because they will try and use the hurts in their life to get closer to the prophet or pastor, using this as an angle for seduction. Through this seduction, they will try to control whoever is in leadership. If you are a man – watch out!

The Jezebel will do her best to infiltrate and be "part of" the leadership. It seems incredible that an apparently spiritually mature person could have a Jezebel spirit working within and through them. The prophetic anointing draws this spirit; it attracts them like moths to a flame.

The Jezebel will do anything to gain control of the pastor. The anointing and the challenge of forbidden fruit attract her, but if she cannot gain control, she will hate him, and do her utmost to destroy him. She will do her best to tarnish his image.

If the person is unwilling to be helped, it may be necessary for them to leave the church. Having left they may continue to speak against you and will look for another Church where she can gain control. *(Some similarities do exist between the Python and the Jezebel spirits).*

You can always test a person to see if they are under the influence of a Jezebel spirit. If the person is taken out of the position of leadership, the Jezebel spirit will react and hate you, because you have taken them out of the controlling position. If it is a woman, whose husband is also in leadership *(or the pastors wife)* she will also take her husband with her *(if possible)* because she is then out to destroy, as she is unable to control any more.

Ahab Spirit Will Allow Jezebel Freedom

If the pastor fails to recognise this, then the Jezebel will be controlling the fellowship and the pastor will be and come under the control of an Ahab spirit. An Ahab spirit *allows* a Jezebel spirit to have control.

The Jezebel will never like the presence of the pastor's wife. She will attack her with great ferocity. She will even accuse her of being a Jezebel! She does this to get the attention away from herself. Undealt with, the Jezebel will become so strong and forceful that she will start praying for the pastor's wife openly, that she needs help, that she needs to change her ways or even that she needs to be removed!

She will also encourage others to pray for her too. Basically this is done so that the Jezebel can get the wife out of the way, so that she can step into her shoes. The Jezebel thinks that she would make a better pastor's wife, and will do her level best to remove the wife completely out of the picture.

You often see in Churches that there seems to be a strong and dominant female. This person will be so special and highly respected, they will have an anointing and they will be moving in amazing signs and wonders, prophesying Godly prophecies here, there and everywhere, and yet can suddenly switch and do something equally deceiving.

These people need to be taught. Their strength needs to be challenged by the leadership, because they have not been discipled in the right way, they have no understanding of what is happening. Their perspective of truth is that if they are right, then everyone else must certainly be wrong!

Therefore lack of submission will come, because they believe that what they have is the latest revelation from God. They do not only deceive others, but themselves as well. Satan is not out just to hurt other individuals, but also the person he is using. An individual can be robbed of his divine right, just as Satan robbed the anointing that God gave to Adam. This is why it is necessary for us to be in submission to God.

She will begin to prophesy great things about your future. Again this is FLATTERY and another way of getting close to the anointing. While she is doing this she will also be prophesying bad things about those who are spiritually discerning. She knows that these perceptive and discerning individuals can detect her presence, and therefore will be a danger to her.

Jezebels with their amazing ability to control or manipulate people, usually see themselves as "prophetesses" because they are able to see into the spirit realm and use this gift to their advantage. In fact it is one of the main tools they use to control people's lives. Usually, they tell someone that they have had dreams about them; the dream is usually a bad one.

Jeremiah 23 talks about lying prophets:

The prophets follow an evil course and use their power unjustly.

(Jeremiah 23:10)

This is what the Lord Almighty says, "Do not listen to what the prophets are prophesying to you; they will fill you with false hopes. They speak visions from their own minds, not from the mouth of the Lord."

(Jeremiah 23:16)

I have heard what the prophets say who prophesy lies in my name. They say, "I had a dream! I had a dream!" How long will this continue in the hearts of these lying prophets, who prophesy the delusions of their own minds?

(Jeremiah 23:25-26)

"Indeed, I am against those who prophesy false dreams," declares the Lord. "They tell them and lead my people astray with their reckless lies, yet I did not send or appoint them."

(Jeremiah 23:32)

As we can see from Jeremiah, the Jezebel spirit is able to use her imagination to conjure up dreams and visions, but they are not from God.

She will also tell people that she is a great intercessor, and that the Lord has given her such burdens. This is a big deception; it is another ploy to win people over to her side. She comes across as so spiritual, that only the most spiritually discerning person will be aware of her deception.

The person, who is being controlled by the Jezebel spirit, will probably be unaware of what they are doing, once again because this spirit not only attempts to deceive everyone else but those it inhabits as well.

Bitterness and Rejection Open the Doors

These people tend to be very sensitive to the things of the spirit. They think that everything they "discern" from the spirit realm is from God, **not realising that their sensitivity can also pick-things-up from demons.** But because the Church is so ignorant of the things of the spirit, they do not understand the person, so instead of correcting, teaching and discipline her, they reject her completely. Because of all the rejection from the Church, she will come to the point where she will trust no one; she will also feel very confused and bitter.

Because of all these hurts, they build a wall around themselves, which will be hard to penetrate. **She will no longer trust the words she hears from people, only those she receives herself, directly from the spirit realm.** God is out there somewhere, so she is easily deceived into thinking that everything she receives in her spirit is from God. She also feels that she is the only one who hears from Him.

I do not believe that people go out wishing to be deceived or to deceive others, but circumstances cause them to be open to deception. Also I am convinced that most of us *(at one time or another)* have walked in some agreement with this spirit. Why? For the express reason that all the while we are in this world and walk on planet earth as flesh and blood, we remain surrounded by control on every side. It's the spirit of this world today and it's all around us: seduction, manipulation, flattery and so forth.

We have to keep ourselves holy and unspotted from this world. Every one of us has been influenced by this world, especially during our tender formative years and at some point also been influenced by this same Jezebel spirit. She is of this world's system therefore each of us has been influenced by it at some point. Yet being controlled or seduced by a Jezebel and actually "being" one - are two different things!

I personally have witnessed on many occasions over the years that those who actually end up operating as one (*a Jezebel*), appeared at first hand to be some of the most tender hearted and sincerely committed, talented, gifted people you could have ever met. And it is precisely this reason that can make it so difficult to detect at times. In fact by the time it is detected very often, it has become so strong and established in that person's life that it takes major adjustments and repentance to get that person set free again.

But remember when God gave Jezebel time to repent she stubbornly **refused** *(Revelation 2:20)*. That's because, very often a strong **spiritual stubbornness** also accompanies this spirit, namely P R I D E *(Proverbs 28:25)*.

In Psalm 78:8 it also says, "…a **stubborn and rebellious** generation that did not **set its heart aright** *(prepare its heart)*, and whose spirit was not faithful to God." Stubborn rebellion causes the development of an un-teachable spirit. This occurs when we stop "preparing our hearts" before the Lord and can no longer listen but prefer being "heard" always instead!

It's terribly sad that some of the most potentially remarkable and talented people in the world have fallen prey to this spirit. Sad because *potential always dies when an un-teachable spirit is developed.*

What is the answer then for the Jezebel who does want to repent in time – before she is thrown to the dogs!? Well the only answer for that and for any of us suffering with anything else, like spiritual pride/lust/rebellion/usurping authority and so forth – is to turn to Joel 2:12-13 and see what it says there…

"Turn to me with all your heart, with fasting, with weeping and with morning." So render you heart, and not your garments; return to the Lord your God, for He is gracious and merciful, slow to anger and of great kindness and He relents from doing harm… (NKJ)

"Rending" is a "ripping-out" of our old hearts and crying out for a completely NEW HEART! Just as King David did in Psalm 51:10 where we witness him pouring out his heart in anguish, to the Lord after he had sinned against God during the time he took Bathsheba and conspired to have her husband killed on the front line.

Wash me thoroughly from my iniquity, and cleanse me from my sin… Against You, You only, have I sinned… Behold, You desire truth in the inward parts… CREATE in me a clean heart, O God, and renew a steadfast spirit within me. Do not cast me away from Your presence, and do not take Your Holy Spirit from me… (NKJ)

Note: Just consider the fact that for God to CREATE anything, it would then be completely NEW. Therefore if God created a clean heart in us it would also be completely new… unspotted from our past sins, just as David's whose sin received no mention in the New Testament - because it had been totally forgiven!

To continue: Jezebel will speak about spiritual matters and say, "God said this to me." She will leave no room for anyone else to discern, because she declares out-right, "God SAID." People will feel unable to approach or disagree with her, after all who can argue with God?

The control aspect is there because they will come to you saying "God spoke to me last night and wanted you to do such and such." They have not heard from God, they are trying to speak things into your life, which they believe needs changing, irrespective of God's will on the matter. This, however, is not the same as the situations where someone in the position of authority asks you to do something, which just involves submitting/serving.

Jezebel will Quote Scriptures

This Jezebel spirit uses the Name of God like a trump card or password! She will say "God told me to tell you this…" or "God says you have to do that…" She will quote scripture to back-up these "words." But we need to remember that Satan knows how to use the scriptures. It takes a strong man of God, a pastor with great discernment to discern what is going on and to confront her.

Another characteristic of the Jezebel is that she will have spiritual insight into the governmental affairs of the Church. She will raise opposing views with other people in the fellowship. She will then confront the leadership with these opposing views, backed by a group of people.

She will share and gossip about any problem she knows about. This is to show how important she is, rather than taking the problem before God in prayer. The Jezebel does not understand the importance of praying about problems. What God shares are not to be shouted around, but rather to be brought before God in intercession?

The Jezebel will seek-people-out to join her. They are usually weak people, with little backbone and easily misled. Before long there will be a group of them, who will be very dependent upon her. Those people will not only be dependent upon her, they will be fully under her control. There will not be an area of their lives, which she is not in control of because she will not allow it.

This control does not happen overnight. She is extremely clever in handling people. At first she appears loving and understanding; listening to their problems and seemingly helps them. Gradually she gains full control and they will not even realise it. They will perceive her as being anointed and of God and will do *anything* for her.

The Jezebel always wants to lay hands on people and will actively *seek* people to pray for. She will do most of her ministering in private, so that the leadership of the Church will not realise what is going on.

Her ministry will consist of not only praying, but also counselling and giving words-of-knowledge. People always share more than they intend without realising, so that when she gives them words-of-knowledge, most of it will be from what they have already shared with her.

Another reason for praying in private is so that no one will actually know what she is saying to these people. If they get upset and approach their pastor, when confronted, the Jezebel will completely *deny* everything or say they had misunderstood what she was saying.

She will also pray with people openly. A lot of the time she will use people in her group to pray for, because she knows that they are very sensitive to her ministry. She prefers not to be recorded, so there is never any proof that she was wrong. She will always be right, shrugging the blame onto someone else. She cannot submit to authority and tends to judge the leadership. She prefers to cause division, pulling down individuals, rather than improve situations.

A Jezebel will normally seek new converts rather than mature Christians. This can leave many of these new converts scared and injured for a long time. Because of this bad experience with a so-called prophetic ministry, they will find it hard to yield to a real prophetic gift.

As I have already said, the Jezebel sees herself as a prophetess to the Church. She seeks credibility by re-prophesying other people's prophecies and known facts, as if they are from God.

Note: Prophets - false or otherwise - should note that God holds them accountable for every prophetic word they give.

If you are a leader of a Church and after reading this you recognise that you may have a Jezebel in operation in your Church, do not ignore it. It will not leave until it has completely destroyed you and your Church if possible.

God makes it quite clear in His Word what He feels about leaders putting up with this Jezebel spirit.

I know your record and what you are doing, your love and faith and service and patient endurance, and that your recent works are more numerous and greater than your first one. But I have this against you, that you tolerate the woman (wife) Jezebel, who calls herself a prophetess (claiming to be inspired), and who is teaching and leading astray my servants and beguiling them into practising sexual vice and eating food sacrificed to idols.

(Revelation 2:19-20 AMP)

As leaders it is our responsibility to oversee the Church, to put to flight anything with an agenda to harm. Therefore **if there is a Jezebel in operation amongst the sheep where you are pastoring, recognise that she is only there to steel, kill and destroy the fold, and not add to it,** *(see John 10:10).*

As leaders we are to look after the sheep, keeping the wolves away. We have to protect our sheep and ourselves from this spirit of Jezebel.

But remember,

We do not wrestle against flesh and blood, but against principalities and powers, against the rulers of the darkness of this age, against spiritual hosts of wickedness in the heavenly places.

(Ephesians 6:12 NKJ)

We are to help this person(s) who is being controlled by the Jezebel spirit. If she/he is teachable and willing to be submissive, then she can be freed from the control. If she is not teachable and will not submit, you have no option but to put her out of the Church, in order to protect your people.

> *...**I gave her** (Jezebel) **time** to repent...and she did not repent.*
>
> *(Revelation 2:21 NKJ)*

CHAPTER 7

Jezebel, Influencing the Church

This Jezebel spirit will usually operate through women, because men it seems are unable to cope with the peculiarities and pressures of this spirit. Men, whom this spirit operates in, usually die prematurely. It seems that women are able to cope with the pressure; in fact women seem to thrive on it!

The spirit will not attach itself to a weak insignificant woman; no it will choose a strong and domineering type. *(I am calling the Jezebel, "she" but again it can also be a man).*

It takes time for the maturing of a spirit to take control over a person or a church and when left unchallenged, her influence swells and spreads.

Jezebels not only like to be taken seriously as intercessors but they like infiltrating the intercession groups in order to divide and conquer; throwing a strong and healthy Church into disunity and disorder. As mentioned before the Pastor's wife is particularly targeted where she can fall ill as a result.

Our Motives must be Right

When the time comes to deal with this type of person, you must make certain that your hearts and motives are right. It is all too easy to judge the person whom the spirit inhabits, but it's the spirit *(operating through them)* that needs to be dealt with.

> *Now I beseech you, brethren, mark them which cause divisions and offenses contrary to the doctrine which ye have learned; and avoid them. For they that are such serve not our Lord Jesus Christ, but their own belly; and by good words and fair speeches deceive the hearts of the simple.*
> *(Romans 16:17-18 KJV)*

We must be firm when dealing with this spirit, but it is essential also to show the individual the love and compassion of Christ. As I have already said, if the person is teachable all will be well, otherwise it's necessary to put her out of the Church, so further division can be prevented.

> *Beloved, believe not every spirit, but try the spirits whether they are of God: because many false prophets are gone out into the world.*
> *(1 John 4:1 KJV)*

We must test the spirits to find whether they are of God or not. Once we know the answer, we are not to run away, but we are to confront them and deal with them properly.

Now we are already aware how Jezebel likes to fasten herself to leaders, especially the pastor but also the prophet if and whenever possible.

To see this let's look at an excerpt from **"The Prophetic Ministry" by Ulf Ekman where he says,** "The prophet often responds with isolation in order to protect himself. He needs to take time alone with God as he enjoys being alone with the Lord. However, this can become a sort of life style for him in which he isolates himself from others in the fear that they will reject him.

Preaching requires a tremendous amount of mental energy. I am not referring to seven minutes of meditation, but to a proper meeting. There is often resistance in the spirit and it is necessary to draw upon every available bit of physical and mental energy. Afterwards you can be quite exhausted.

It is at this point that the enemy usually comes. The parasites and critics start to show up. It is easy to be slightly more sensitive and weak after having preached. And because the enemy knows this, this is when he strikes.

Such was the case with Elijah. He had just chopped off the heads of 450 prophets of Baal and seen the fire fall on Mount Carmel. But Jezebel only needed to open her mouth and say, 'You will die in the same way as those prophets, Elijah, and wherever you are, I'm going to find you' *(1 Kings 19:2).*

After being so bold before 450 men, Elijah now trembled before a woman. But she was not just any other woman; a spirit of death had been released through her against the prophetic anointing of Elijah. He ran away and hid, went into isolation and wished he were dead.

This sort of isolation is self-chosen and unhealthy. It is something which you must be aware of, especially if you stand in the office of a prophet" *(Page 148, The Prophetic Ministry, Ulf Ekman, printed by Enbloms Grafiska, Uppsala, Sweden 1990).*

No church has immunity from Jezebel. In fact the bigger the church, the more she will try to infiltrate. She will go-all-out to take control and manipulate. In her bid to reach the top, she won't care whom she hurts on-route.

The stronger you're anointing, the more spiritual attacks you are going to get. Oddly enough, the anointing attracts the Jezebel. But not content with that, she will "pick off" the weak members of the Church also.

Satan can send a ministry into the church seeming so fantastic, at ease with the supernatural, with signs and wonders following and yet it can be a Jezebel spirit! When this happens, there will be no submission to authority or to the leadership; neither will there be any foundation in their lives *(they might look good in the pulpit, but have questionable personal lives that they want to keep hidden).*

They will not actually join a church, until they know they are accepted and a part of the leadership. Within a short space of time the Jezebel will have attracted a large number of people around her. *(People can have similar mannerisms as these and not have a Jezebel spirit – so be careful NOT to make it a witch-hunt!)*

Lying Signs and Wonders

It is by their fruits that you will know them, not by their spiritual ability.

Beware of false prophets, which come to you in sheep's clothing, but inwardly they are ravening wolves. Ye shall know them by their fruits. Do men gather grapes of thorns, or figs of thistles? Even so every good tree bringeth forth good fruit; but a corrupt tree bringeth forth evil fruit.

A good tree cannot bring forth evil fruit, neither can a corrupt tree bring forth good fruit. Every tree that bringeth not forth good fruit is hewn down, and cast into the fire. Wherefore by their fruits ye shall know them.
(Matthew 7:15-20 KJV)

It is by the fruit of their character and ministry, not by the size of the signs and wonders they perform; this stops us being duped by lying signs and wonders (*2 Thessalonians 2:9*).

There are a lot of people in the church today, who have been given too much liberty. They're doing stuff they should not be doing; nevertheless because their leadership are ignorant about Jezebel, they are getting away with it.

It's time to train people properly so that knowledge is developed along with spiritual discernment and the ability to deal with this type of deceiving spirit.

Jezebel Hates the Prophetic Gift

Why does Jezebel hate the prophetic gift? Because the prophet is an anointed "seer," who can see what is *really* going on and posses the greatest threat to her more than any other gift. The prophet is the first to "hear" from God about what is going on in the nations and the first to "see" any oncoming attacks of the enemy.

Not only does Jezebel try to unite herself to the prophet and pastor in the spirit realm, she wants to unite with them physically as well, wherever possible. This is part of her overall seduction.

Still the prophet has the spirit of Elijah and has a heart for the restoration of the family, but Satan wants to kill that. The prophet has a heart for God and is looking to restore His order and structure within the Church, the five-fold ministry and the family.

God is looking for them to be re-established but Satan is out to destroy them, and he will use Jezebel's "sexual attraction" to help destroy Church life and the family.

Note: This is where a Python and Jezebel spirit differ – there is less sexual attraction with the Python. But Satan will use Jezebel's sexual charms to the max!

The Greatest Threat

All across the Nations, Satan has targeted prophets. He has sent Jezebels *(both immoral women and homosexuals)* to seduce and destroy them. The greatest threat to the Jezebel is the prophet. Likewise the greatest threat to the prophet is the Jezebel. *(Again we know that only Jezebel could strike fear into the heart of Elijah 1 Kings 19:3).*

Jezebel as the wife of King Ahab, worshipped Baal the god of Phoenicia. She encouraged Ahab to build shrines to worship this god and anyone who spoke against it was put to death, along with the prophets of God.

Jezebel's main opposition came from Elijah, he held a contest on Mount Carmel *(1 Kings 18:20-40)*, to prove that his God was the true God. After this, Jezebel was all out to kill Elijah. She had no respect for other people's property, this was shown when she heard that her husband, Ahab, desired Naboth's vineyard in Jezreel. She had Naboth stoned to death.

The spirit of Jezebel is the same today; she is still out to destroy the prophets of the true God. She will take anything she desires; she is a liar, a thief and a murderer. *(Jezebel is a **lascivious spirit** – promoting lust without restraint & greed that can't be satisfied).*

According to 1 John 2:14 there are three basic weaknesses that we are given to in this world: the lust of the flesh, the lust of the eyes, and the pride of life. In other words two thirds of all human weakness centres on "LUST."

> *For all that **is** in the world, the lust of the flesh, and the lust of the eyes, and the pride of life, is not of the Father, but is of the world.*
>
> *(see 1 John 2:14 KJV)*

Here is an excerpt from a book called "The Unique Woman," co-written by Ed and Nancy Cole some years ago, but still relevant today.

"It seems today there is a secondary 'ozone layer' made by a spirit of lust that covers the earth. It is like fissionable fallout material that touches everyone everywhere to some degree or another. Soap-operas on the TV seem to thrive on sex, crime and violence. It seems as if the spirit of television is a spirit of lust. Modern day romance novels also cater to lustful appetites. Fornication, or sex sin, is another of the five sins. The church has not been immune. Sex sins have been the problem of the church in the 1980's.

Women serving as **temple prostitutes** are not found just in the Old Testament, but they are a New Testament affliction of the Church as well. Of course we are too nice, too enlightened and sophisticated, too couth and cultured, too religious to admit that the women we read about, who are having affairs with ministers are oftentimes nothing more than temple prostitutes. They lust after men of God rather than seeking God, and oftentimes are thinking that they are doing God 'service' by servicing men of God.

Lesbianism among women leaders in the world today also has had an effect on all society. Once a deeply distressed man wanted to talk to me for counsel, he was suffering terribly since his wife left him. When he told she had run off with one of their best friends, I asked, 'What was he like?' He whispered, 'It wasn't a he...'

Talk about the emasculation of manhood in the world today! He was experiencing it first-hand. Losing your wife to another man is not uncommon, but losing her to another woman is devastating. The same devastation can come from homosexuality. What must it be like for the woman whose husband, 'comes out of the closet,' confesses he is homosexual, insists he can be bisexual, states he wants to continue the marriage, and wants her to share his love with another man?

It was hard for me to come to grips with the fact that women have sexual addictions that are as strong as or stronger than men's. The world's 'Chippendale' syndrome is a reality – fanatically addicted women worshipping the male phallus, willing to lose all virtue and without shame, succumbing to their basest lusts.

The great deception of our day is thinking you can practice an immoral lifestyle and still be in right relationship with God. No one who abides in Christ can habitually practice sin *(1 John 3:6)*.

To say you cannot live without abiding in sin is to deny the power of the resurrection. The Spirit of Holiness that raised Christ from the dead can still enable men and women to lead 'overcoming' lives.

There is a difference between someone who commits a sin and someone who practices sin. Whether the sex sin is an image of the mind, a perverted philosophy that justifies a moral aberration or an unclean habit, it needs to be admitted, confessed, repented of and forsaken" *(Pages 32-33, Edwin Louis Cole and Nancy Cole, The Unique Woman, published by Honour Books, Tulsa, Oklahoma USA 1991).*

❖

CHAPTER 8

Living Without Restraint

Ulf Ekman while studying to be a priest in Uppsala, Sweden, said, "One of the professors invited a number of homosexuals – 'Christian' homosexuals, as they referred to themselves. They were asked to talk about the positive aspects of homosexuality to a group of between 200-300 prospective priests.

A small group of us knew that they were coming, so we took some time that morning to pray. We took authority over the spiritual forces, which lie behind homosexuality."

Do not lie with a man as one lies with a woman; that is detestable.

(Leviticus 18:22)

Because of this, God gave them over to shameful lusts. Even their women exchanged natural relations for unnatural ones. In the same way the men also abandoned natural relations with women and were inflamed with lust for one another. Men committed indecent acts with other men, and received in themselves the due penalty for their perversion.

(Romans 1:26-27)

Pastor Ekman said, "This section of our education was nothing other than the **seduction** of future priests to accept homosexuality as a genuine form of love. It was then hoped that they would go on to spread that opinion in churches throughout the country.

However, homosexuality is not a genuine display or expression of love. According to the Word of God, it is an abomination in the eyes of God. Of course, just as with every other abomination, it is possible to be delivered from homosexuality. The blood of Jesus cleanses from all sin, when this sin is confessed. If evil spirits are involved, they can be cast out and the person can be set free."

"The moment I set foot in the room," Ulf Ekman said, "I noticed that for some reason the professor looked slightly shaken. He was upset and grumpy. It was obvious that the spirit powers, which we had bound, were now disturbed.

This group of five homosexuals began to talk about how 'fantastic' it was to be a homosexual and just how Christian it was. Afterwards we had the opportunity to ask questions. Because I could feel myself boiling inside, I asked the Lord, *'Should I say something now?'* **'No,'** He replied.

Someone stood up to say something which was basically correct, but which seemed to be said at the wrong time and therefore dropped to the ground like a dry leaf. They were the right words, but at the wrong time and it was obvious that they had no effect.

Then another stood up and said something generally apologetic about how hard and dogmatic Christians had been and how we really should be more understanding and loving. They were the wrong words at the wrong time.

I sat praying quietly in tongues the whole time. Then I asked the Lord, *'Should I say something now?'* **'No,'** He said, 'You need to calm down a little bit.' So I just sat and waited... *'Should I say something now?'* I asked. **'No!'** He said. *'Now?'* I asked. **'Yes!'** He finally responded, **'I want you to say it now...'** Then I stood to my feet and put up my hand."

Right Words, Right Time

"I was given the floor, so I turned to the first chapter of Romans and read what it says there about homosexuality. Then I said, 'You say that homosexuality is talked about only in the Old Testament and that the New Testament has nothing to say about it, but just seems to accept it. But here in Romans 1:27 is the same word which is used in Leviticus 18:22; the word 'abomination.' The Word of God says that it is not at all acceptable, but that it is an abomination.'

I did not raise my voice or shout or prophesy; I just spoke calmly, lead by the Hold Spirit. When I said this, the entire auditorium exploded. The Word of God came into the room like a hammer. The otherwise cultivated, aesthetic, humane, humanistic professor had suddenly become a different man. What was really inside him suddenly came out; he became angry and irritated.

Someone else began to speak and I felt God telling me to request the right to reply. It was a panel discussion, so I said, *'Right to reply!'* When I did, this polite, intellectual professor screamed from across the room, *'No! He has been given enough time already!'*

Their intention had been to come and neatly seduce us all, but now their plans had come to nothing. I did not stand up and say, *'Thus says the Lord,'* but said, *'I'd like to read a scripture.'* This scripture acted as a spear, a sword and a lance, which caused total chaos. The professor completely lost his head and several others turned to and shouted, *'How lacking in love!'*

They tried to interrupt the whole discussion. I wondered to myself, *'What should I do now?'* They had virtually begun to jump on top of me. Then I sensed the Lord telling me, 'Go forward and shake hands with one of the homosexuals and tell them that I love him.' So I went up, extended my hand and said, *'Jesus loves you!'*

'I'm not touching your hand,' he said. *'If I had my way, I would spit in your face.'* *'That wouldn't matter,'* I said. *'You can do that if you like, but you need to know that Jesus loves you anyway. He loves you and He has a wonderful plan for your life.'* I just stood there, speaking the love and freedom of God to him; *'You can be set free; you can be released from this bondage.'*

As I said these things, I could feel my knees shaking. There was such a confrontation in the spirit world.

If you were to examine this whole situation on a superficial level, you might feel, *'How terrible! Things were really stirred up. It couldn't have been God since people got so disturbed.'* But God is present even in the middle of disturbances. The following semester they did not dare to hold a public discussion. Instead, the students were divided up into smaller groups. But even then there were people in each of the small groups who stood up for the Word of God."

Treachery on Every Level

Pastor Ekman concludes, "This treachery is taking place today in schools, companies and within political debates, not just regarding homosexuality, but also the New Age movement and occultism. **Wherever you look you will discover this 'sophisticated' form of seduction.** Some Christians have even become so sophisticated that they too have swallowed these things. It is time that we stood up and kicked the devil out of every single area where he has found an entrance.

There is no reason why we should have to follow the devil's rules. God plays according to different rules. If the devil presents himself politely, intellectually and seductively, you can prophecy in the broadest dialect and say, *'Thus says the Lord!'* God looks at the heart! **God is looking for prophets who will prophesy in the Holy Spirit and not just run around getting angry at people or with no more than personal opinions to shout about everything"** *(Pages*

172-176, The Prophetic Ministry, Ulf Ekman, printed by Enbloms Grafiska, Uppsala, Sweden 1990).

We've spoken about the division that Jezebel can cause. But let me point out again here that in Jezebel's endless quest to seduce men and women of God – when found out and confronted will ALWAYS say it was the other way round! Counter-accusing and twisting truth is Jezebel's art form.

However I'll say it again, the greatest sexual seduction this insidious spirit specializes in is destroying godly marriages! Creating a lasting breach between godly spouses is a "top-trophy." One subtle tactic is to get couples to use sex in terms of "reward & punishment," *(withdrawing sex or giving sexual rewards in order to get one's own way!)* Such behaviour as this; using sex as a crude bargaining-tool or as a manipulative-leverage with in the marriage, is a far cry from the behaviour spoken of in 1 Peter 3:1-6 where it says:

In like manner you married women, be submissive to your own husbands – subordinate yourselves as being secondary to and depending on them and adapt yourselves to them. So that even any do not obey the Word [of God] they may be won over not by discussion but by the [godly] lives of their wives.

When they observe the pure and modest way in which you conduct yourselves, together with your reverence [for your husband. That is, you are to feel for him all that reverence includes] – to respect, defer to revere him; [revere means] to honour, esteem, (appreciate, prize), and [in the human sense] adore him; [and adore means] to admire praise, be devoted to, deeply love and enjoy [your husband].

Let not yours be the [merely] external adorning with [elaborate] interweaving and knotting of the hair, the wearing of jewellery or changes of clothes; but let it be the inward adorning and beauty of the hidden person of the heart, with the incorruptible and unfading charm of a gentle and peaceful spirit, which (is not anxious or wrought up, but) it is very precious in the sight of God.

For it was thus that the pious women of old who hoped in God were (accustomed) to beautify themselves, and were submissive to their husbands, adapting themselves secondary and dependent upon them.

It was thus that Sarah obeyed Abraham (following his guidance and acknowledging his headship over her by) calling him lord – master, leader, authority. And you are now her true daughters if you do right and let nothing terrify you – not giving way to hysterical fears or letting anxieties unnerve you (AMP).

It has to be said, that **if you are married and your partner wants to make love with you, you should NOT refuse.** Such refusal is only acceptable, when praying and fasting and when the woman is on her menstrual-cycle.

The wife does not have authority over her own body, but the husband does. And likewise the husband does not have authority over his own body, the wife does. Do not deprive one another except with consent for a time, that you may give yourselves to fasting and prayer; and come together again so that Satan does not tempt you because of your lack of self-control.

(1 Corinthians 7:4-5 NKJ)

God says in His Word, **not to withhold yourself from one another**. The authority of His Word is higher then your authority because without the Word you have no foundation, the Word is your foundation. The Bible says quite clearly that a woman will desire her husband *(Genesis 3:16)*. If you do not desire your husband, you have a problem *(ask the Lord to "give" you that desire or to restore it to your heart)*.

❖

CHAPTER 9

Encouraged to Fornicate

L et me add something here before I continue. It seems in the world today, that when one is setting out in life as a young male or female, every bit of encouragement that one might need to fornicate - is readily available! TV, peer pressure, school, radio, MTV, lyrics in popular songs, even most of today's advertising campaigns!

All of them thrust the sex message: *"DON'T withhold yourself... loose your virginity, be free, express yourself, be 'normal,' don't be frigid, do what comes naturally, flow with the chemistry, 'HAVE SEX!' Whenever, wherever with whomever - as long as it 'feels' right and you remember to be SAFE!"*

It's got to be said, that in today's world, if a young school leaver, leaves school with no other qualifications, at least they've learnt how to have "...*SAFE SEX!*" But what a legacy we have left our children, what a warped set of priorities we are teaching the up and coming generations. It's true, sadly that today, in our schools our young people, only in their early teens are being so freely informed about sex, to the extent that it is really teaching them *"how"* to go about it!

Okay so young "horny" teenagers hardly need any encouragement in these matters and if no one talked about it in the schools, I'm not suggesting that they wouldn't get up to it anyway – they would. But while some are more than ready to indulge their senses, even get home tutoring of a sort, from older siblings, there are others who are just NOT ready. We have to ask the question, are we allowing the introduction of our youngest and dearest to the world of sex before they're ready?

Trusted School System

Satan cleverly uses the "trusted" school system, to cunningly seduce the young out of their innocent ignorance into full blown promiscuity by informing and convincing them in a sophisticated and educated manner that it's OKAY, because times HAVE changed. *It's "OLD-SCHOOL" to think any other way.* **"Be progressive, come to an educated decision, let nothing stifle your freedom, be properly informed, know the risks, take the right precautions, let go... have sex and lose your virginity quick...!"**

Through the guise of EDUCATION our youth have been encouraged into promiscuity - whether ready or not – dulling their natural sense of caution. The agenda that's pushed sounds something like this: "If you do it safely, then it eliminates the risks and if there's no risks, then there's no need for fear." **Scripted and clever propaganda that recognizes where there is no fear – there's no "restraint."** So from the world's point of view, all efforts are employed to open our youth *"wide"* – not for the Gospel - but for abuse!

Some would defend the current situation with this type of argument, *"Oh but you fundamentalists are stifling our youth; they need to 'express-themselves' and be free! Leave them alone… don't you realise that your legalistic world view is the problem here – lighten up!"*

Fundamental? YES! Legalistic? NO! God also wants us to be FREE and enjoy life to the full. Sex is not sin; it is a blessing *(1 Timothy 6:17b)*, **a marriage gift from God, especially for married couples *(opened on the wedding night - not before!)*** Once opened it must be enjoyed and kept sacred before Him.

Sex could have been painful - similar to childbirth, solely for procreation purposes *(of necessity only!)* But God didn't do things that way - He created the orgasm!

Let's Be Real About It

Everything created by God is GOOD. Satan didn't create it, just perverts it. The origin of the orgasm is God and His goodness towards us. He wanted us to enjoy reproduction! Replenish the earth, subduing it and multiplying – was a good prospect, not a bad one! Besides He had to encourage us to multiply some how otherwise this world would have a very limited population indeed!

From the beginning of creation until now, God cares about every detail of our lives! He cared that Adam was alone – He saw that it was not good. This means that God literally seeks our good… and nothing of our lives escapes His notice!

Just imagine, a world without colour, taste or smell? But God has given us all such things to enjoy and gets joy Himself watching us relish what He created. The flowers, the scenery, good food, aroma, flavours and textures! Just think how we grind fresh coffee beans because they smell and taste so fantastic! Then there's the sweet smoothness of chocolate! God definitely cares about detail and provided us with endless variety of choice – even allowing us room for personal preference! Nothing is bland. In its original glory – all of God's creation reflects His brilliance!

Nevertheless people have become *"lovers of pleasure rather than lovers of God."* They have used what has been created against its Creator! We should enjoy life WITH God not in-spite of Him or even worship His creation instead of Him! Do we worship beauty only to deny its artist? What paradox!

And in this tender goodness of God, whose plan involved our fulfilment – also created a special "safety-net" with which to surround sex: the boundary and institute called marriage.

But from a very impressionable age we are sold the lie: **"You must experiment, sow your oats, gain 'experience' to find out whose sexually compatible before settling on a partner for life…!"**

WHAT A LIE. WHEN DO YOU STOP EXPERIMENTING? HOW MANY TIMES MUST YOU "TEST" BEFORE DECLARING SOMEONE SEXUALLY COMPATIBLE? **Where does that end up, how far does it go?**

It is in all these things that young or single people need to put their faith and trust fully in God and decide **"God is their source, for *everything* including the compatibility of their future partner."** This does require real TRUST, but we either trust God or we don't and if we do, then we will be prepared to wait until He reveals who, where and when – through prayer and confirmation.

Experimentation and Promiscuity

Experimentation and promiscuity only leads to confusion, comparisons, hurts, and a whole host of other abuses. Instead of sex being the pleasure that God intended for it to be *(in the intimacy of a beautiful relationship)* it becomes an ongoing cycle of pain, hurt and abuse.

Do we really want to play the harlot with this world's system by allowing our children to be prostituted, taught in the school of fornication rather than the school of the Holy Spirit? The result will burden successive generations with a harvest from such fornication: abuse, hurt, pain, division, divorce, infidelity, child abuse and pornography. Including illegitimacy; wounded and orphan-spirits.

Revelation 2:20 reveals the intent of this unclean spirit Jezebel as spiritual deception. Prophetess and seductress - educating and enticing people to commit sexual sins... as was her aim then and is now.

To teach... fornication (sexual immorality) (KJV emphasis added).

At this point I want to make a clarification here, that **teaching our children about sex is not wrong! Of course not...** But we should have a whole different agenda than that of the world, which is PREPARATION FOR "MARRIAGE" NOT PROMISCUITY! **We are taught through scripture to seek first the Kingdom of God and therefore this goes for our children as well. Righteousness in everything, including our relationships...**

Right Time - Right Place

Parents who love their children will help to nurture what's right in them and help them to find what's best for them including teaching them to wait for the right timing and right place. **Sex has a "right time & a wrong time! A right place and a wrong place" and we must teach our children to recognise, distinguish and discern the difference between right and wrong – even though the world around them fails to see the difference!**

This is where "Sexual Education" in our schools, on TV and the likes of the MTV music culture, has a lot to answer for. It's an adult world. Some secondary schools go as far as issuing condoms and demonstrating their use, *"just in case!"*

I dare say that, as Christian parents we see a LINE here! There's a whole lot of difference between "informing" than "aiding and abetting!" I am sure most parents *(whether Christian or otherwise)*, after discussing this delicate subject of sex with their children, wouldn't dream of demonstrating or issuing a small stock of condoms for random occasions! Ludicrous.

What a confused message this gives: *"Green light or red Mum and Dad... ?!"*

❖

CHAPTER 10

New Age Seduction

The seduction of women is top priority on Satan's hidden agenda for the Church. But in this chapter we will look mainly at how New Age has infiltrated society, including the Church.

Wanda Marrs says in her startling book, "New Age Lies To Women" *(this is perhaps the first to completely reveal the New Age campaign to deceive and seduce women)*. Satan knows that if he can capture the mind and body of a woman, he then can quickly move to conquer her husband, her children, her entire family and circle of friends.

She thoroughly documents the almost incredible plan of the New Age leadership to foster sexual immorality by inciting lust feelings and creating seductive imagery in women's minds. She also explains how the **New Age**

has successfully been able to damage and hurt women psychologically, break up marriages, lure our children into Satanism, cults and the occults, kill unborn babies and undermine women's faith in God.

Wanda says in her book *(Page 107, Wanda Marrs and Texe Marrs, New Age Lies to Women, published by Living Truth Publishers, Austin, Texas USA 1989)* that the Mother Goddess *(Semiramis)*, "was also called the Queen of Heaven. She bedecked herself with jewels and gold and spread the doctrine that those who followed her and were initiated into the 'Mysteries' would be prosperous, gain abundant material wealth, and enjoy sexual ecstasy as spiritual gifts from gods.

Drunkenness and merriment was a prime feature of worship as revellers lifted their cups and chanted praises to the goddess. Sexual orgies then followed a revealing of the Mysteries, the secretive, satanic doctrines that were taught by Babylonian priests and priestesses. Today, the sexual ritual and licentiousness of Babylon are back, introduced into modern-day society by the New Age."

It is interesting that in Italy, a country devoted to the Catholic Church, and committed to worship of Madonna is also a country steeped in sexual immorality. As one who has lived in Italy for some years, I can certainly affirm that she is a country filled with fornication, prostitution, pornography, adultery, promiscuity and lust; sun worship, worship of the body, beauty and ultimately the worship of s e x.

I remember when a friend and I visited the Vatican in Rome *(sightseeing)* for the first time, to our horror and disbelief we discovered that only yards from the Vatican itself, there were magazine stands selling all kinds of very explicit pornography! This came as a real culture shock for us, but it also revealed the stark reality of just how warped a society can become, when these two extremes can exist together side by side and be considered expectable, commonplace normality. There's nothing NORMAL about that...!

The deception of it so grieved me, because that which so many around the world deem as "Holy & Pure" *(the Vatican)* could be so openly ignorant of such perversity and fornication within its immediate vicinity. What deception? Just think, one could go to the most famous Church in the world, with the most famous Pastor in the world *(Pope!)* just to buy your selves some pornography on the way out... crazy!?

Sexually Suggestive and Occult Scenes

Violence, illicit sex and the occult seem to go hand in hand in many rock songs. "Heavy-metal groups take their listeners ever further out. One group, Judas Priest, on their album, 'Defenders of the Faith,' sing 'Eat Me Alive,' the words depicting a girl being forced at gun point commit oral sex.

Even more explicit are the words of songs by groups like W.A.S.P. For example, the lyrics of one of their songs speaks of pictures of naked ladies lying on the bed and the smell of sweet convulsion and about howling in heat and finally, about committing the sex act, like a beast" *(Page 70, Jay Cocks, Richard Stengel and Dennis Worrell, Rock is a Four Lettered Word, published by* TIME *Magazine, Tampa, Florida USA Sep 30, 1985).*

Another clear example of the negative moulding power of pop idols are the recent claims by a child-pornography expert. In report to the United Press International, Judith Reisman said the following:

"Pictures encourage child pornography. You're dealing with an idol or heroine who carries with her a great deal of power and symbolism. For example, Madonna is seen as a desired being in society, so all young women want to be desired; they want to achieve. If the nude pictures are described in popular magazines as appropriate, desirable behaviour, then youngsters, both girls and boys, will construe that to be the case. Large numbers of them will. Thus the pictures will encourage voluntary displays by youngsters. This is not good."

"As far as the negative sexual problems, one news-magazine reported that women all too often are portrayed as 'bimbos.' They undress in silhouette, stretch out over car hoods and snarl like animals. Their dress includes fishnets and leathers" *(Women in a Video Cage, page 54).*

Madonna – Pop Goddess of the 80's

In 1989 Madonna's hit video "Like a Prayer" was replete with religious imagery and blasphemous overtones. The video begins in a church setting as Madonna sensually caresses the feet of a statue of a black Catholic saint. The icon sheds tears and comes to life. She picks up a dagger, touches the blade and the palms of her hands begin to bleed, emulating the superstition of *stigmata (a supernatural event which many erroneously believe signifies God's blessing upon an individual).*

Madonna dances in a field of burning crosses in little more than a slip and is seductively kissed by the "saint" character. There is even a scene implying lesbian activity on the church's altar with a choir member!

High advertising mobiles hung in record stores across America, which peddled the "Like a Prayer, LP" with the inscription, "Lead Us Not To Temptation." Though the singer went as far as to have "patchouli," a West Indian Fragrance, mixed with the packaging glue for the "Like a Prayer" records and tapes, the marketing technique employed by Madonna and her publicist, Liz Rosenberg could hardly cover up the stench the video created (*USA Today, March 30th, 1989. PDI*).

Is this practice being restored today by the New Age? Below is the incredible, yet commonplace, true account of one women's modern-day return to the religious depravity of Mystery Babylon, (*Pages 75-90, Rickie Moore, A Goddess In My Shoes, published by Humanics New Age, Atlanta, Georgia USA 1988*).

"I know spiritual did not exclude sexual. The Tantrum and Taoist approaches to spiritual sexuality appealed to me.

When I heard they emphasised the need for a man to keep the woman absolutely satisfied, I said sign me up! I wanted to become an enlistee.

We started off slowly, going to every available workshop, buying all the books written about it and setting aside time...

Our first tantra course paid off. Now... I can have a 'jade garden' or a 'lovely lotus,' if I choose. His male body part became a magic sceptre, a healing wand, or… jewel. Just singing, 'The jewel or the lotus' was a turn on.

Through successive heights of ecstasy, we began to see visions with our minds, fill them with out hearts and dream them simultaneously.

Yoga had prepared us individually for what we were experiencing together.

I was, perhaps the daughter of a thousand shining stars… the Shakti, the potent female energy that can change the face of earth… the portal to the past and the future, a sanctuary for incarnating souls, a pleasure field of heaven, a sweet and beautiful flower, complete with perfume and nectar, surely worthy of being worshipped and kissed.

I thanked the stars then for all little girls, witches and crazy ladies… and for all little boys, wizards and holy men. I didn't need anyone to tell me I was a goddess… I knew it!

We began our ceremony at home… the altar was adorned with happy yellow flowers, and bright burning candles that illuminated pictures of our loved ones. A single, long stemmed rose, my symbol for protection, reminded us that we could experience the mystical union with the universe…

We stood naked in front of the altar… then we took a comfortable tantra seat and gazed long and deep into each other's eyes…

Then, he was on his knees in front of me… I stood there looking holy and goddess-like in my new exotic belt."

Sex will be Prominent in the End Times

The New Age Movement is capturing tens of thousands of woman's souls through sexual lies. Sex, of course is a big draw throughout society. Sexual images and erotic fantasies permeate our lives. We cannot turn on our television set or open the pages of a newspaper or a women's magazine without coming face-to-face today with the graphic nature of sexual enticements and inducements. The New Age has mastered the act of inciting lust and unbridled passion in the breast of women.

Wanda Marrs says, "This is a religion that has as its core the same unholy practices that were prevalent in Babylon, Egypt, Rome, Greece and throughout the orient. In the centuries before Christ, and in the first centuries after Jesus' first coming, history is replete with the story and descriptions of the fertility rites and the sexual favours granted by high priestesses in the temple of such cities as Corinth, Athens, Ephesus and Memphis...

Initiates celebrate the sex act with temple prostitutes, many of whom came from the aristocratic class – from the very cream of society. In Ephesus and elsewhere, the cult of Diana encouraged sexual license and sacred promiscuity. The idolatrous state of Diana depicted her with a multitude of breasts, signifying her sensual nature. In Egypt, the sensual nature of the mother goddess, Isis, was also worshipped in fertility rites.

Babylonian Queen of Heaven

Hislop wrote that Semiramis, the Babylonian 'Queen of heaven,' led a licentious life and gave birth to many illegitimate children. Yet, the people grew to worship her as the 'Holy Virgin.' In the Goddess religions, it was thought that sacred and ritual sex cleansed and purified; therefore the term 'Virgin' was used, though it's meaning is far different than that envisioned by Christians."

Note: Alexander Hislop (Born at Duns, Berwickshire, 1807; died Arbroath, 13 March 1865) was a Free Church of Scotland minister infamous for his outspoken criticisms of the Roman Catholic Church. He wrote several books, his most famous being The Two Babylons: Papal worship Revealed to be the worship of Nimrod and His wife.

"The Roman emperors Nero and Caligula, who professed belief in Roman Gods derived from the Mystery cults of Babylon and Pergamos, were given to sexual orgies and incredible acts of debauchery and sexual depravity.

Homosexuality and pederasty *(child abuse)* was rampant throughout the Roman Empire and especially in Greece where the normal practice of heterosexuality *(male-female)* was even sneered at by many of the affluent class and nobility...

Remember the New Agers who practice Tantric yoga actually believe that sexual union – in or out of marriage – brings spiritual communion with the divine energy forces of the Universe. Those involved in witchcraft and Satanism consecrate themselves to Satan through ritual sex orgies.

Marilyn Ferguson, in the New Age classic 'The Aquarian Conspiracy,' enthusiastically reports that for many New

Agers, sex outside of marriage is the wave of the future. She says that the traditional view of fidelity and 'one man-one woman' has given way to more 'liberated' views. Quoting sociological experts, Ferguson adds that the New Age generation is free from guilt over sex.

Promotion flyer, '1987 International Seth Seminar,' Seth an international network of groups composed of disciples of 'Seth,' a demon, channelled by psychic Jane Roberts, teaches that 'the universe is of good intent; evil and destruction does not exist... we create our own reality – literally – through the beliefs we hold, and therefore can change what we don't like.' In a recent leaflet published by the Seth Centre, the group stated it's main ideas regarding sex as follows:

We are in this to enjoy ourselves – spirit, mind and body. If it isn't fun, stop doing it! ... It is natural to be bisexual. Heterosexuality, homosexuality, and lesbianism are equally worthwhile and valid sexual orientations... There is no authority superior to the guidance of a person's inner self" *(Pages 57-59, Wanda Marrs and Texe Marrs, New Age Lies to Women, published by Living Truth Publishers, Austin, Texas USA 1989).*

❖

Conclusion

To wrap things up, "those the son sets free are free indeed" we must never take our eyes off of Jesus!

There are many agendas in the world and in the Church - some of which have been highlighted throughout this book. Specifically speaking the "Python" and "Jezebel" both wreak havoc because they know that the anointing comes from-the-top-down - not from the bottom-up!

Leaders however are not the only ones targeted by seduction of course and there are many avenues and victims of seduction. The New Age themes weave their way throughout our education systems, all forms of entertainment and church life. Producing false prophecies, visions and words – nothing short of DIVINATION *(something the python spirit specializes in)*.

"As we were on our way to the place of prayer... a spirit of divination *(python)*... kept following" this revealed an affinity that the python seeks with the apostolic ministry and prayer. Why? Because prayerful apostolic leaders are dangerous, when their preaching is empowered with prayer it can effectively break open the spiritual "gateways" of any city.

Sophisticated world-humanism likes to take-on the TRUTH of God's Word, but God's Word says, "I warn everyone who hears the words of the prophecy in this book: If anyone adds anything to this, God will strike him... If anyone takes away any words from this book of prophecy, God will take away his portion of the tree of life..." *(Revelation 22:18-19 GW)*

Daniel 11:32, "...such as violate the covenant he shall pervert and *seduce with flatteries,* but the people who know their God shall prove themselves strong and shall stand firm and do exploits." We have nothing to fear if we stay within what God has said to us. But once we step beyond our given boundaries we are easily seduced by flatteries.

"I have a few things against you, because you allow that woman Jezebel... to teach and seduce..." *(Revelation 2:20)* We must make sure that we don't give way to her teachings. "The Spirit expressly says that in latter times some will depart from the faith, giving heed to deceiving spirits and doctrines of demons..." *(1 Timothy 4:1 NKJ)*

Homosexuality is not just an orientation or sexuality but a "premeditated-government-agenda." As one particular site revealed, "global controllers have resorted to any means necessary to reduce population - including adding sterilants to water supplies & promoting homosexuality" who carried the article, "Slow kill Holocaust proof the Government is Poisoning you," which exposed facts concerning extreme governmental efforts to curb population growth as published by the Planned Parenthood-World Population, NYC, NY, 19.70. *(See www.infowars.com also www.static.infowars.com/2011/12/i/ article-images/jaffememo-watersterilants.pdf)*

Ultimately **submission to authority** is our ultimate safety net, "...when the righteous are in authority *(become great)*, the people rejoice; but when the wicked man rules, the people groan" *(Proverbs 29:2 NKJ)*. And no matter what agenda the world has - God is always GREATER. He has made EVERY provision for His children to be obedient and successful in and for His Kingdom *(Isaiah 1:19)*.

❖

Bibliography

- Bevere, John. <u>Thus Saith the Lord?</u> (90, 120) Lake Mary, Florida USA: Published by Creation House, A Division of Strang Communications Company. Copyright © 1999

- Cocks, Jay, and Richard Stengel, and Dennis Worrell. <u>Rock is a Four Lettered Word.</u> (70) Tampa, Florida USA: Published by TIME Magazine. Copyright © Sep 30, 1985

- Cole, Edwin Louis, and Nancy Cole. <u>The Unique Woman.</u> (32-33) Tulsa, Oklahoma USA: Published by Honor Books. Copyright © 1991

- Ekman, Ulf. <u>The Prophetic Ministry.</u> (148, 172-176) Uppsala, Sweden: Published by Enbloms Grafiska. Copyright © 1990

- Hölé, J. Konrad. <u>The Making of a Cutting Edge Leader.</u> (4) Minneapolis, Minnesota USA: Published by The World Press. Copyright © 1997

- Hölé, J. Konrad. <u>You were Born a Champion, Don't Die a Looser!</u> (31) Minneapolis, Minnesota USA: Published by The World Press. Copyright © 1997

- Maddux, Bob. <u>Fantasy Explosion.</u> (84) Ventura, California USA: Published by Regal Books, A Division of G.L Publications. Copyright © 1986

- Marrs, Wanda, and Texe Marrs. <u>New Age Lies to Women.</u> (57-59, 107) Austin, Texas USA: Published by Living Truth Publishers. Copyright © 1989

- Moore, Rickie. <u>A Goddess in My Shoes.</u> (75-90) Atlanta, Georgia USA: Published by Humanics New Age. Copyright © 1988

- Schlink, M. Basilea. <u>New Age.</u> (8-10) Darmstadt, Germany: Published by The Evangelical Sisterhood of Mary. Copyright © 1988

- Strong, James. S.T.D., L.L.D. 1890. Strong's Exhaustive Concordance; Dictionaries of the Hebrew and Greek Words. e-Sword ® version 7.6.1 Copyright © 2000-2005. All Rights Reserved. Registered trade mark of Rick Meyers. Equipping Ministries Foundation. USA www.e-sword.net.

- Unless otherwise indicated, all scriptural quotations are from the HOLY BIBLE, NEW INTERNATIONAL VERSION ®. NIV ®. Copyright © 1973, 1978, 1984 by the International Bible Society. Used by permission of Zondervan Publishing House. All rights reserved.

- Scripture quotations marked AMP are taken from The Amplified Bible. *Old Testament* copyright © 1965, 1987 by Zondervan Corporation, Grand Rapids, Michigan. *New Testament* copyright © 1958, 1987 by The Lockman Foundation, La Habra, California. All rights reserved.

- Scripture references marked GW are taken from GOD'S WORD®, © 1995 God's Word to the Nations. Used by permission of Baker Publishing Group.

- Scripture references marked KJV are taken from the King James Version of the Bible.

- Scripture references marked NKJ are taken from the New King James Version. Copyright © 1982 by Thomas Nelson, 1982 by Thomas Nelson, Inc. Used by permission. All rights reserved.

- Scripture references marked RSV are taken from the Revised Standard Version of the Bible, copyright 1952 [2nd edition, 1971] by the Division of Christian Education of the National Council of the Churches of Christ in the United States of America. Used by permission. All rights reserved.

❖
Ministry Profile

Doctor Alan Pateman, an apostle, is the President and Founder of **"Alan Pateman Ministries International"** (APMI), which was established in England back in 1987, a Christian-based *(parachurch)* non-profit and non-denominational outreach. This ministry is now focusing in two main areas: First **"Connecting for Excellence"** Apostolic Networking (CFE) and secondly, the teaching arm, **"LifeStyle International Christian University"** (LICU).

CFE is a multi-facetted missions organisation with the purpose of connecting leaders for divine opportunities and building lasting relationships, to touch the lives of leaders literally the world over. Apostle Dr Alan Pateman has to date ordained more than 500 ministers in over 50 NATIONS. In addition there are ministries, churches and schools who are in Association or Affiliation, looking to him for apostolic counsel and oversight.

Secondly LICU, which was founded in 2007, is a study program to help people discover their purpose and destiny. A global network of university campuses and correspondence students, demonstrating the Supernatural Kingdom of God through Doctrinal, Apostolic and Prophetic Teaching. Dr Alan holds the position of President/CEO, Professor of Theology, Biblical Studies and Apostolic Ministry. LICU is exploding throughout Europe, Asia and Africa, enhancing the Body of Christ

Dr Alan has authored more than 35 books including numerous teaching materials and LICU university courses (30) along with hundreds of Truth for the Journey articles on kingdom lifestyle *(that are regularly distributed globally via the internet).*

He is recognised as an Apostle, Bishop, Leadership Mentor, University Educator, Motivational Speaker, Connector and Author, who has also been featured on national and international TV and radio networks throughout the years.

Currently Apostle Alan, his wife Dr Jennifer reside in Lucca *(Tuscany)* Italy and travel out from their Apostolic Company.

- Alan Pateman Ph.D., D.Min., D.D., M.A., B.Th.

Academic Background

Dr. Alan Pateman attended several colleges throughout his training *(including studying Theology at Roffey Place, Horsham, UK and a Member of Kerygma - with Rev. Colin Urquhart and Dr. Bob Gordon - 1985-1987)* before being awarded a Doctorate of Divinity *(2006)* in recognition of his lifetime achievements by the International College of Excellence, now "DanEl Christian College" *(President: Dr. Robb Thompson USA)* also "Life Christian University" *(Dr. Douglas Wingate USA)* where he also earned a Bachelor of Theology B.Th. *(2006)*, a Master of Arts in Theology M.A., a Doctor of Ministry in Theology D.Min., *(2007)* and Doctor of Philosophy in Theology Ph.D. *(2013)* from LICU.

❖

To Contact the Author

Please email:

Alan Pateman Ministries International

Email: apostledr@alanpateman.com
Web: www.AlanPatemanMinistries.com

*Please include your prayer requests
and comments when you write.*

❖

Other Books

Media, Spiritual Gateway

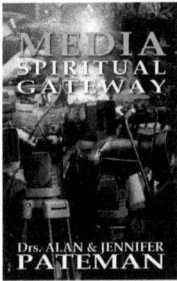

Let's face it; we live in the era of fake news! It's always existed, but never been quite so prominent. Today it's an all-out-war between fact and political fiction.

ISBN: 978-1-909132-54-2, Pages: 192, Format: Paperback, Published: 2018 *Also available in eBook format!*

Millennial Myopia, From a Biblical Perspective

The standard for every generation is Jesus. However Millennial Myopia describes the trap of focusing everything on one particular generation or demographic cohort, at the exclusion and expense of all others. The Church cannot afford to make this mistake too.

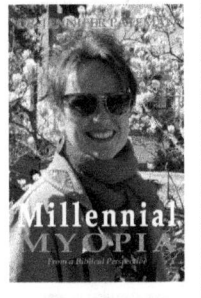

ISBN: 978-1-909132-67-2, Pages: 216, Format: Paperback, Published: 2017 *Also available in eBook format!*

Truth for the Journey Books

TONGUES, Our Supernatural Prayer Language

In writing to the church at Corinth, Paul encouraged them to continue the practice of speaking with other tongues in their worship of God and in their prayer lives as a means of spiritual edification. "He that speaketh in an unknown tongue edifies, charges, builds himself up like a battery."

ISBN: 978-1-909132-44-3, Pages: 144,
Format: Paperback, Published: 2016
Also available in eBook format!

Seven Pillars for Life and Kingdom Prosperity

I submit these "Seven Pillars for Life and Kingdom Prosperity" to you, (Love, Prayer, Righteousness, Obedience, Connections, Management, Money). It's my desire that you walk in the triumphs that God has ordained for you.

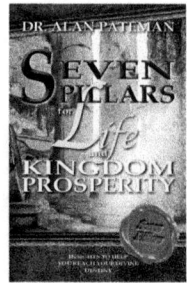

ISBN: 978-1-909132-46-7, Pages: 220,
Format: Paperback, Published: 2016
Also available in eBook format!

WINNING by Mastering your Mind

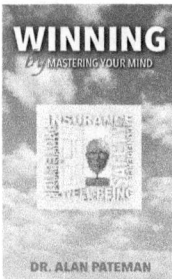

Someone once said, "Happiness begins between your ears and your mind is the drawing room for tomorrow's circumstances..." Remember, what happens in your mind will happen in time, and therefore one of our first priorities must be mind-management.

ISBN: 978-1-909132-40-5, Pages: 136,
Format: Paperback, Published: 2017
Also available in eBook format!

Truth for the Journey Books

Kingdom Management for Anointed Prosperity

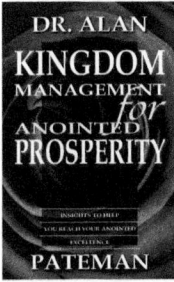

In his book, "Kingdom Management for Anointed Prosperity," Dr. Alan Pateman reveals how we can avoid living in continual crisis due to mismanagement. Life happens to all of us, but how we handle it matters most.

ISBN: 978-1-909132-34-4, Pages: 144, Format: Paperback, Published: 2015
Also available in eBook format!

Why War: A Biblical Approach to the Armour of God and Spiritual Warfare

Spiritual warfare means different things to different people, but from a biblical standpoint Ephesians 6:10-18 gives us the best biblical definition of spiritual warfare possible. We can also see how God has thoroughly equipped us for victory not just self defence!

ISBN: 978-1-909132-39-9, Pages: 180, Format: Paperback, Published: 2013
Also available in eBook format!

Forgiveness, The Key to Revival

Scripture is absolute when it comes to forgiveness. IF we forgive, THEN we are forgiven. It's that simple but no one said it was easy! Nonetheless, forgiveness can be likened to a spiritual key that unlocks spiritual doors and opportunities!

ISBN: 978-1-909132-41-2, Pages: 124, Format: Paperback, Published: 2013
Also available in eBook format!

Truth for the Journey Books

Revival Fires - Anointed Generals
Past & Present (Part Two of Four)

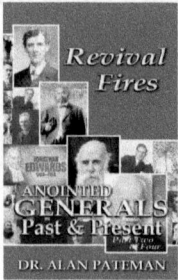

Seasons might be changing but God's Word remains the same. The heart of the author is to help train, equip and be a blessing to those men and women who will be willing to fulfil their potential in ministry and be properly equipped for service.

ISBN: 978-1-909132-36-8, Pages: 142,
Format: Paperback, Published: 2012
Also available in eBook format!

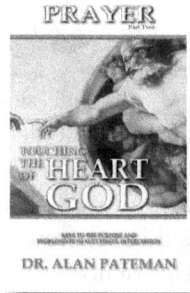

Prayer, Touching the Heart of God (Part Two)

Touching the Heart of God is the very essence of prayer. Whether we are petitioning God with very specific requests or consecrating ourselves before Him and rededicating our lives - whatever the case may be – the true essence of all praying is "Touching the Heart of God."

ISBN: 978-1-909132-12-2, Pages: 180,
Format: Paperback, Published: 2012
Also available in eBook format!

Prayer, Ingredients for Successful Intercession
(Part One)

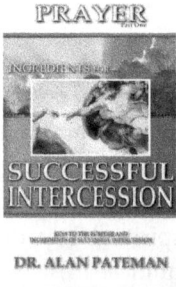

This Book is the first of two books on Prayer. Dr. Pateman provides an exhaustive study, showcasing the vital ingredients necessary for all successful prayer. An excellent power-packed teaching tool, either for the individual or for the local church prayer group, that's eager to lay a solid foundation but don't know where to start!

ISBN: 978-1-909132-11-5, Pages: 140,
Format: Paperback, Published: 2012
Also available in eBook format!

Truth for the Journey Books

Apostles: Can the Church Survive Without Them?

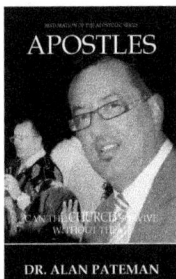

Before Jesus returns a significant increase of the anointing will be poured out on the Body of Christ, but can the Church handle such an anointing? *(Acts 5:5)* Billy Brim once said, "As much as the anointing is powerful to create, it is as powerfully destructive of evil." The fear of God will be restored with the apostolic and people will begin walking with such anointing, as we have never seen before!

ISBN: 978-1-909132-04-7, Pages: 164,
Format: Paperback, Published: 2012
Also available in eBook format!

Sexual Madness: In a Sexually Confused World

This book discusses the sensitive subject of political correctness in our world today and the growing fear of causing offence in the public arena. It also discusses the rise of homosexuality, pedophilia and all other forms of sexuality, as there are many. Including modern statistics on pornography.

ISBN: 978-1-909132-02-3, Pages: 160,
Format: Paperback, Published: 2012
Also available in eBook format!

His Life is in the Blood

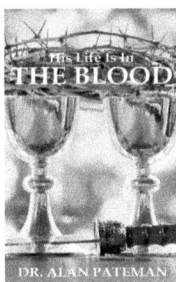

Blood is the trophy of every battle. The spilt blood of Jesus Christ is our trophy. It is our freedom from sin and bondage. Nothing can enter the blood-bought temples of the Holy Ghost! This book will encourage you to apply the blood of Jesus our Passover Lamb to your life, just as the children of Israel did in the Old Testament. Not merely talking or reading about it, but applying it.

ISBN: 978-1-909132-06-1, Pages: 152,
Format: Paperback, First Published: 2007
Also available in eBook format!

LIFESTYLE UNIVERSITY

Raising Up
Christian Leaders

Dear Friends,

Have you considered becoming one of our international students? We are privileged to welcome you, from around the world, to "LifeStyle International Christian University" *(the teaching arm of Alan Pateman Ministries International).* **An English speaking university** dedicated to your success; to see you trained and equipped to fully succeed in your God given Destiny.

It is our passion to raise up the leaders of tomorrow, who will have influence in all realms of authority, including the Body of Christ. Men and women of strategy, wisdom and true godliness, who'll stand with stature and maturity in this hour.

It's undeniable that in today's world, recognised education has become indispensable, therefore it is our desire to offer well balanced and well structured courses. Those that have been written by gifted and talented ministers of God, who seek to be inspired by God's Holy Spirit.

Consequently we have put together a **flexible curriculum,** designed both for correspondence students and campuses, which is a strategy to reach the distant learner; whether provincial, national or international. In fact we have many correspondence students from around the world, including a growing number of successful campuses, in various countries.

This is a growing platform, where men and women of dignity and passion, can grow and be established in their God given endeavours. As God is the healer of the nations, we pray and believe that many of our alumni will go on to **become world changers** in their own right.

We are proud of each and every one of our LICU students.
It would be our pleasure if you would join them on this incredible journey!

Doctor Alan Pateman

Alan Pateman Prof. Ph.D., D.Min., D.D., M.A., B.Th.
PRESIDENT AND CEO
www.licuuniversity.com www.cfeapostolicnetwork.com
Email: info@licuuniversity.com   Mob: +39 366 329 1315

For more information visit our website/facebook or contact our office, using the details below:

Website: www.licuuniversity.com
Facebook: www.facebook.com/LICUMainCampus
Email: info@licuuniversity.com
Telephone: +39 366 329 1315

All Books Available

at

APMI PUBLICATIONS

Email: publications@alanpateman.com
*Also Available from Amazon.com
and other retail outlets.*

*If you purchased this book through Amazon.com
or other and enjoyed reading it, or perhaps one of
my other books, I would be grateful if you could
take a couple of minutes to write a Customer
Review, many thanks.*

www.ingramcontent.com/pod-product-compliance
Lightning Source LLC
Chambersburg PA
CBHW071540040426
42452CB00008B/1075